WJEC GCSE

ENGLISH

 ROGER LANE

Teacher's Guide

ENGLISH
ENGLISH LITERATURE
ENGLISH LANGUAGE

WJEC
CBAC

OXFORD
UNIVERSITY PRESS

UNIVERSITY PRESS

Great Clarendon Street, Oxford OX2 6DP

Oxford University Press is a department of the University of Oxford.
It furthers the University's objective of excellence in research,
scholarship, and education by publishing worldwide in

Oxford   New York

Auckland   Cape Town   Dar es Salaam   Hong Kong   Karachi
Kuala Lumpur   Madrid   Melbourne   Mexico City   Nairobi
New Delhi   Shanghai   Taipei   Toronto

With offices in

Argentina   Austria   Brazil   Chile   Czech Republic   France   Greece
Guatemala   Hungary   Italy   Japan   Poland   Portugal   Singapore
South Korea   Switzerland   Thailand   Turkey   Ukraine   Vietnam

Oxford is a registered trade mark of Oxford University Press
in the UK and in certain other countries

British Library Cataloguing in Publication Data

Data available

ISBN 978-0-19-831084-6

10 9 8 7 6 5 4 3 2

Printed in Great Britain by Bell and Bain Ltd., Glasgow

Contents

Introduction

Section 1: Reading

Section 2: Writing

Section 3: Speaking and Listening

Course Overview

WJEC GCSE English is a complete course for students and teachers taking either the WJEC English Language and English Literature GCSEs or the single WJEC English GCSE. It caters for all levels of ability and offers complete support for Controlled Assessment and examinations through a range of activities, resources and sample reading, writing and speaking and listening assessments. All of the materials have been carefully matched to the unit requirements of the three specifications.

Course components

The course consists of the core Student Book (suitable for students at all levels), the Foundation Student Book (suitable specifically for Foundation students), this Teacher's Guide, the interactive OxBox CD-ROM and three Skills & Practice Books to help students achieve their potential in the three GCSEs.

The OxBox CD-ROM

- Includes many further activities and lesson ideas, including editable worksheets and presentations to supplement the Student Book and Teacher's Guide.
- Provides interactive activities, including some with Record & Playback functionality, ideal for speaking and listening work.
- Includes grids, sample questions and example responses from the Student Book in editable format.
- Contains ready-made and customizable course and lesson plans; the lesson player helps you arrange and launch the resources you want to use in sequence.
- You can add your own resources, using easy-to-follow instructions.
- OxBox user management facility allows you to easily import class registers and create user accounts for all your students.

The Student Book

- A single book for all three specifications.
- Each chapter begins with a clear explanation of the examinations or Controlled Assessments covered in each chapter. Colour-coded icons help students to distinguish which information relates to GCSE English, English Language or English Literature.
- Examiner's Tips are provided throughout, giving students valuable pointers on how to perform to their best ability.
- Students are encouraged to evaluate their progress through self-assessment checklists.
- Each chapter contains a number of activities, culminating in exam and Controlled Assessment practice tasks. These are followed by sample student responses with Examiner's Comments, to allow students to better understand what is required of them and identify ways to gain a higher mark.

Skills & Practice Books

- Structured to match the specifications exactly, so students have a clear idea of what is required of them.
- Guides students through exam question types and Controlled Assessment tasks, ensuring that all necessary skills are covered.
- Includes lots of clear, useful advice from senior examiners.
- Each unit includes a 'Boost your grade' section, ensuring students at all levels are given the opportunity to maximize their potential.

Using this Teacher's Guide

This Teacher's Guide aims to save you time and effort, offering a wealth of support for delivering the material in the Student Book, and steering you through the course with straightforward advice, answers, and lesson ideas.

For each chapter of the Student Book, this Teacher's Guide provides:

separate teaching notes for each relevant specification

a clear explanation of specification demands and Assessment Objectives

key ideas covered in the corresponding chapter of the Student Book

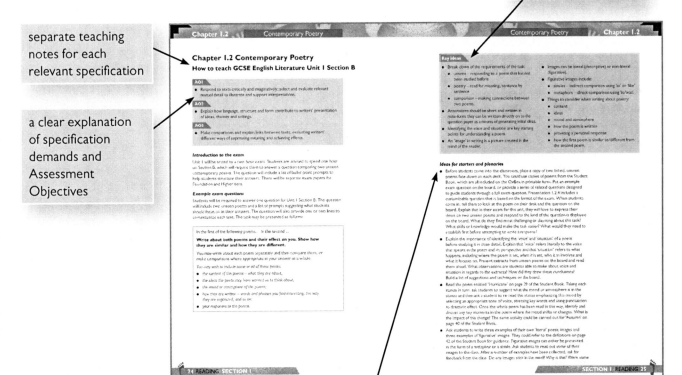

examples of exam questions and Controlled Assessment tasks

lesson ideas and suggestions for starters and plenaries

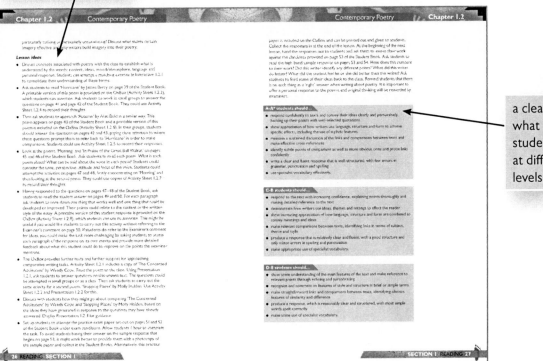

a clear guide to what is expected of students performing at different grade levels

Matching the Specification: WJEC GCSE English

The WJEC GCSE English specification consists of four units.

Unit	Outline	Student Book	Teacher's Guide	Other Components
Unit 1: **English in the daily world (reading)**	Exam 1 hour 40 marks 20%	Chapter 1.1	Chapter 1.1b	Foundation Book: Chapter 1.1 OxBox CD-ROM: English Unit 1 English Skills & Practice Book: Unit 1
Unit 2: **English in the daily world (writing)**	Exam 1 hour 40 marks 20%	Chapter 2.2	Chapter 2.2b	Foundation Book: Chapter 2.2 OxBox CD-ROM: English Unit 2 English Skills & Practice Book: Unit 2
Unit 3: **English in the world of the imagination Section A - Literary texts**	Controlled Assessment 40 marks 20%	Chapter 1.3 Chapter 1.4 (Different Cultures text only)	Chapter 1.3a Chapter 1.4b	Foundation Book: Chapters 1.3, 1.4 OxBox CD-ROM: English Unit 3 English Skills & Practice Book: Unit 3
Unit 3: **English in the world of the imagination Section B - Open writing**	Controlled Assessment 40 marks 20%	Chapter 2.1	Chapter 2.1b	Foundation Book: Chapter 2.1 OxBox CD-ROM: English Unit 3 English Skills & Practice Book: Unit 3
Unit 4: **Speaking and Listening**	Controlled Assessment 40 marks 20%	Chapter 3.1	Chapter 3.1b	Foundation Book: Chapter 3.1 OxBox CD-ROM: English Unit 4 English Skills & Practice Book: Unit 4

Matching the Specification: WJEC GCSE English Language

The WJEC GCSE English Language specification consists of four units.

Unit	Outline	Student Book	Teacher's Guide	Other Components
Unit 1: **Studying written language**	Exam 1 hour 40 marks 20%	Chapter 1.1	Chapter 1.1a	Foundation Book: Chapter 1.1 OxBox CD-ROM: English Language Unit 1 English Language Skills & Practice Book: Unit 1
Unit 2: **Using written language**	Exam 1 hour 40 marks 20%	Chapter 2.2	Chapter 2.2a	Foundation Book: Chapter 2.2 OxBox CD-ROM: English Language Unit 2 English Language Skills & Practice Book: Unit 2
Unit 3: **Literary reading and creative writing Section A - Studying written language**	Controlled Assessment 40 marks 15%	Chapter 1.3 Chapter 1.4 Chapter 1.5		Foundation Book: Chapters 1.3, 1.4, 1.5 OxBox CD-ROM: English Language Unit 3 English Language Skills & Practice Book: Unit 3
Unit 3: **Literary reading and creative writing Section B - Using language**	Controlled Assessment 40 marks 15%	Chapter 2.1	Chapter 2.1a	Foundation Book: Chapter 2.1 OxBox CD-ROM: English Language Unit 3 English Language Skills & Practice Book: Unit 3
Unit 4: **Spoken language Section A - Using language**	Controlled Assessment 40 marks 20%	Chapter 3.1	Chapter 3.1a	Foundation Book: Chapter 3.1 OxBox CD-ROM: English Language Unit 4 English Language Skills & Practice Book: Unit 4
Unit 4: **Spoken language Section B - Studying spoken language**	Controlled Assessment 20 marks 10%	Chapter 3.2	Chapter 3.2	Foundation Book: Chapter 3.2 OxBox CD-ROM: English Language Unit 4 English Language Skills & Practice Book: Unit 4

Matching the Specification: WJEC GCSE English Literature

The WJEC GCSE English Literature specification consists of three units.

Unit	Outline	Student Book	Teacher' Guide	Other Components
Unit 1: **Prose (different cultures)** **and poetry (contemporary)** **Section A -** **Individual texts in context**	Exam 1 hour 30 marks 21%	Chapter 1.4	Chapter 1.4a	Foundation Book: Chapter 1.4 OxBox CD-ROM: English Literature Unit 1 English Literature Skills & Practice Book: Unit 1
Unit 1: **Prose (different cultures)** **and poetry (contemporary)** **Section B -** **Comparative study**	Exam 1 hour 20 marks 14%	Chapter 1.2	Chapter 1.2	Foundation Book: Chapter 1.2 OxBox CD-ROM: English Literature Unit 1 English Literature Skills & Practice Book: Unit 1
Unit 2: **Option A - Literary heritage drama and contemporary prose**	Exam 2 hours 60 marks 40%	Chapter 1.5	Chapter 1.5a	Foundation Book: Chapter 1.5 OxBox CD-ROM: English Literature Unit 2 English Literature Skills & Practice Book: Unit 2
Unit 2: **Option B -** **Contemporary drama and literary heritage prose**	Exam 2 hours 60 marks 40%	Chapter 1.5	Chapter 1.5b	Foundation Book: Chapter 1.5 OxBox CD-ROM: English Literature Unit 2 English Literature Skills & Practice Book: Unit 2
Unit 3: **Poetry and drama** **(Literary heritage)**	Controlled Assessment 40 marks 25%	Chapter 1.3	Chapter 1.3b	Foundation Book: Chapter 1.3 OxBox CD-ROM: English Literature Unit 3 English Literature Skills & Practice Book: Unit 3

About Controlled Assessment

Various elements of all three GCSE English specifications are examined through Controlled Assessment. Unlike the examined units, the Controlled Assessment units are not split into Foundation and Higher tiers.

The idea behind this system of assessment is for students to produce an original response without the drawbacks of 'over-preparation' and the complications for teachers of ensuring candidates' work is authentic. It allows centres to have a greater degree of control, selecting when learners complete the assessment. Tasks can be completed at any point in the academic year, provided they meet the deadline for submission.

The stages of Controlled Assessment

Controlled Assessment takes place in a series of stages:

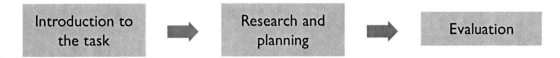

Introduction to the task

During this phase, the teacher introduces students to the task to ensure they understand exactly what is required of them. (You may wish to use the specification outline presentations on the OxBox to support you.)

Research and planning

During this part of the process, students are able to work under limited supervision, and may make use of research materials. They may work collaboratively, and you may also give them general advice (although you may not comment on their preparatory work). However, if you provide them with worksheets or other support documents related to their assignments, you will need to include copies of these in the folders sent to the external moderator.

Evaluation

Students write their final piece of work or take part in a speaking and listening activity, and perform these tasks in controlled conditions and within a specified time limit. The time allocated to each written task may be split between more than one session, but students must not have access to their work outside of the sessions. They may take one A4 side of their own notes into the assessments, but this must not include a plan or draft essay. Further guidance on notes can be found on the WJEC website at: http://www.wjec.co.uk/uploads/publications/10285.pdf.

Curriculum planning: Notes from Roger Lane

Below is an example of possible course planning, which you may find useful. There are other examples available and you will of course plan according to the needs of your students and school.

The course has been broken down initially into teaching and assessment components. These are often part-units. They have been re-labelled with a letter A - K to avoid ambiguity.

The three summaries of assessment have been laid out in full on the next pages. There follows an example of a course structure for a joint English Language/English Literature course, but with an English course in mind for those candidates for whom a switch would be expedient.

There is also an example of a course outline for a one-year post-16 English Language course.

Priorities

- Cross-over pieces to cater for 'doubtful' literature candidates.
- Controlled Assessments time-table along 'coursework' lines; exams as final assessments.
- Early coverage and/or entry for some, most, or all candidates.

ENGLISH LANGUAGE (planned with English Literature)

A   **Unit 1**   **Non-fiction reading**   **20%**   **1hr exam 3 - 6 weeks**

Planning criteria: Close links with Unit 2? Part of final exam(s)? Benefits of maturation?

To consider: Complete exams early.

CROSS-OVER TO ENGLISH UNIT 1

B   **Unit 2**   **Information and ideas: writing**   **20%**   **1hr exam 3 - 6 weeks**

Planning criteria: Close links with Unit 2? Part of final exam(s)? Benefits of maturation?

To consider: Complete exams early.

CROSS-OVER TO ENGLISH UNIT 2

C   **Unit 3 (part)**   **Extended literary text**   **15%**   **2hrs CA 6 - 8 weeks**

Planning criteria: To be completed adjacent to study of same text for lit CA/exam.

To consider: Complete textual studies early.

SOME CROSS-OVER TO ENGLISH UNIT 3 (DIFFERENT CULTURES TEXTS ONLY)

D   **Unit 3 (part)**   **Creative writing**   **15%**   **2hrs CA 3 - 4 weeks**

Planning criteria: Familiar territory for students or students need benefit of maturation.

To consider: Early completion.

SOME CROSS-OVER TO ENGLISH UNIT 3 (IF 1ST AND 3RD PERSON WRITING BOTH COVERED)

E	**Unit 4 (part)**	**Individual presentation**	1/3 of 20%	2 - 3 weeks (or integrated)

Planning criteria: Link to written expression? Integrated? Assessments of individual contributions.

To consider: Leave Speaking and Listening assessment until late in course?

CROSS-OVER TO ENGLISH UNIT 4

F	**Unit 4 (part)**	**Group discussion**	1/3 of 20%	2 - 3 weeks (or integrated)

Planning criteria: Link to understanding (reading/literature) skills? Assessments of pair/group work.

To consider: Leave Speaking and Listening assessment until late in course?

CROSS-OVER TO ENGLISH UNIT 4

G	**Unit 4 (part)**	**Role-play**	1/3 of 20%	2 - 3 weeks (or integrated)

Planning criteria: Link to drama study and/or transactional writing? Assessments of role-plays.

To consider: Leave Speaking and Listening assessments until late in course?

CROSS-OVER TO ENGLISH UNIT 4

H	**Unit 4 (part)**	**Studying spoken language**	10%	2hrs CA	3 - 4 weeks

Planning criteria: Some benefit in leaving until Y11? Linked to Speaking and Listening? Part of final 40%?

To consider: Complete all Controlled Assessment in Y10 or complete as part of final 40% when left alongside Unit 3

ENGLISH LITERATURE (planned with English Language)

I	**Unit I**	**Different cultures prose**	21%	2hrs exam	6 - 8 weeks*
		Unseen contemporary poetry comparison	14%		3 - 6 weeks

*Planning criteria: Strong possibility of use as extended lit text in Eng Lang; *aggregate time could be reduced for different cultures prose; unseen poetry flexible.*

To consider: 35% total value - not likely to be used as final assessment.

SOME CROSS-OVER TO ENGLISH UNIT 3 (DIFFERENT CULTURES TEXTS ONLY)

J	**Unit 2a/b**	**Heritage prose/drama**	20%	2hrs exam	6 - 8 weeks
		Contemporary prose/drama	20%		6 - 8 weeks

Planning criteria: Favourite for end of course; two stand-alone text choices; could return to text used previously in extended literary text used for English Language.

To consider: The only single unit worth the full 40% for the end-game assessment; other routes would require two units to be assessed at end

K   Unit 3   Linked Shakespeare/   25%   4hrs CA   6 - 8 weeks
heritage poetry

Planning criteria: Full half-term required; good way of committing students to the course early.

To consider: Could be done early and stored

CROSS-OVER TO ENGLISH UNIT 3

The joint English Language and English Literature course could possibly run for 11 half-terms and approximately 63 weeks.

ENGLISH (stand-alone, but with cross-overs in mind)

A   Unit 1   Non-fiction reading   20%   1hr exam   3 - 6 weeks
Planning criteria: Close links with Unit 2? Part of final exam(s)? Benefits of maturation?

To consider: Complete exams early.

CROSS-OVER TO ENGLISH LANGUAGE UNIT 1

B   Unit 2   Information and ideas: writing   20%   1hr exam   3 - 6 weeks
Planning criteria: Close links with Unit 2? Part of final exam(s)? Benefits of maturation?

To consider: Complete exams early.

CROSS-OVER TO ENGLISH LANGUAGE UNIT 2

C   Unit 3 (part)   Linked Shakespeare/   10%   4hrs CA   6 - 8 weeks
heritage poetry

Planning criteria: Full half-term required.

To consider: Could be done early and stored.

CROSS-OVER TO ENGLISH LITERATURE UNIT 3

D   Unit 3 (part)   Different cultures prose   10%   2hrs CA   6 - 8 weeks
Planning criteria: Full half-term required.

To consider: Complete textual studies early; store for final submission.

SOME CROSS-OVER TO ENGLISH LITERATURE UNIT 1 (DIFFERENT CULTURES TEXTS ONLY)

E   Unit 3 (part)   Creative writing   15%   2hrs CA   3 - 4 weeks
Planning criteria: Familiar territory for students <u>or</u> students need benefit of maturation.

To consider: Early completion.

SOME CROSS-OVER TO ENGLISH LANGUAGE UNIT 3 (IF 1ST AND 3RD PERSON WRITING BOTH COVERED)

| **F** | Unit 4 (part) | **Individual presentation** | **I/3 of 20%** | **CA** | **2 - 3 weeks** |

Planning criteria: Link to written expression? Integrated? Assessments of individual contributions.

To consider: Leave Speaking and Listening assessment until late in course?

CROSS-OVER TO ENGLISH LANGUAGE UNIT 4

| **G** | Unit 4 (part) | **Group discussion** | **I/3 of 20%** | **CA** | **2 – 3 weeks** |

Planning criteria: Link to understanding (reading/literature) skills? Assessments of pair/group work.

To consider Leave Speaking and Listening assessment until late in course?

CROSS-OVER TO ENGLISH LANGUAGE UNIT 4

| **H** | Unit 4 (part) | **Role-play** | **I/3 of 20%** | **CA** | **2 – 3 weeks** |

Planning criteria: Link to drama study and/or transactional writing? Assessments of role-plays.

To consider: Leave Speaking and Listening assessments until late in course?

CROSS-OVER TO ENGLISH LANGUAGE UNIT 4

The stand-alone English course covers between 27 and 40 weeks of work.

An example of initial planning for a joint English Language/English Literature course

Term I > Term 2

D   Creative writing

Some misgivings about lack of maturation, but no real justification for agonizing. Get it done with a crisp teaching unit.

K   Linked Shakespeare/poetry

Commit students to English Literature course. But also allows for cross-over to English.

F   Group discussion (Non-functional)

An early assessment done in conjunction with linked assignment.

Term 2 > Term 3

C   Extended literary text/different cultures prose

Definitely want to link this to Literature Unit 1 exam. And everything crosses-over to English so far!

I   Lit exam I   Different cultures prose/unseen poetry comparison

Summer Year 10; Literature assessment 35%, now 60% of course covered.

Term 3

H   Studying spoken language

A light term for new pieces because of diversions and catch-ups, but get this done cleanly.

Completed in Year 10:

English Language:	**D** 15%; **C** 15%; **F** third part of 20%; **H** 10%	(40%+)
English Literature:	**K** 25%; **I** 35%	(60%)
English:	**D** 20%; **K** 10%; **F** third part of 20%; **C** 10%	(40%+)

Term 4 > Term 5

A   Non-fiction reading

A strong teaching module preparing students for January or June.

B   Information and Ideas: writing

Still worth linking it to above, despite free-standing units.

E   Individual presentation (Functional)

Assessments can be woven in or done discretely.

G   Role-play (Functional)

Assessments can be woven in or done discretely.

English Language and English requirements covered by Winter Term YII.

Term 5 > Term 6

J   Heritage/contemporary prose/drama

Set texts study. Final 40%.

An example of a one-year English Language course

Term 1 > Term 2

D   Creative writing

Get to know the students.

C   Extended literary text

Get the long text out of the way.

F   Group discussion

Probably chance to link to the above.

Term 2 > Term 3

H   Studying spoken language

Finish the Controlled Assessments.

E   Individual presentation (Functional)

Possibly link to exam practice.

A   Non-fiction reading

Exam practice now definitely in focus.

G   Role-play (Functional)

Link to exam practice.

Term 3

B   Information and Ideas: writing

End strongly with writing skills.

Chapter 1.1a Non-Fiction Texts
How to teach GCSE English Language Unit 1

AO3

- Read and understand texts, selecting material appropriate to purpose, collating from different sources and making comparisons and cross-references as appropriate.
- Develop and sustain interpretations of writers' ideas and perspectives.
- Explain and evaluate how writers use linguistic, grammatical, structural and presentational features to achieve effects and engage and influence the reader.
- Understand texts in their social, cultural and historical contexts.

Introduction to the exam

Unit 1 will be assessed by an exam lasting one hour. Students will be provided with two non-fiction texts and will be asked to answer four questions on them. Some of these questions will ask students to focus on the first text and some of them will ask students to focus on the second text. The fourth question will ask students to compare and contrast both texts.

The non-fiction texts may include fact-sheets, leaflets or letters; or extracts from autobiographies, diaries, advertisements, reports, articles, webpages and brochures. The material will always include visual elements such as images, diagrams or the use of particular layout features.

There will be separate Foundation and Higher tier papers.

Example exam questions

All questions will test reading for understanding and meaning. Some questions will require students to read each source text and pick out relevant information. Higher tier questions may be worded as follows:

- According to this article, why/what/who/when…
- According to the writer of this letter, what/why/who/when…
- What is the writer's opinion of…
- What are the writer's thoughts about…

Foundation tier questions may provide additional support, such as suggesting how many points the student should aim to make in his or her answer. These questions may be worded as follows:

- List **ten**… mentioned in the brochure that are….
- List **three**… that take place in…
- List **four** of the facilities available in…
- List **ten** reasons given in the article for…

On Foundation and Higher tier papers, one question will ask students to focus on 'how' the writer of one of the texts achieves a particular effect. The effect stated in the question might be to interest, persuade, instruct or advise the reader. The questions may be worded as follows:

- How does the writer try to make his/her website/article interesting for his/her readers?
- How does the brochure/website persuade readers that…?
- How does the writer reveal the…?

- The writer of the article/letter/website/advertisement tries to… how does he/she do this?

For both papers, Question 4 will test the student's ability to compare both source texts. Questions may be presented as follows:

- Compare and contrast what… and… say about…
- Both of these texts are about… compare and contrast the texts.

Question 4 may also include a short bullet-point list of prompts suggesting what students should focus on in their answer.

Key ideas

- Different reading skills required:
  - location and reorganization – finding and rewording information
  - inference – reading 'between the lines'
  - appreciation of style – the way the author writes.
- When reading it is important to firstly identify the audience, purpose and format of the text.

- Things to think about when considering the voice of the text:
  - texts that use direct address, speak directly to the reader
  - texts can be written in a formal or informal tone
  - imperative verbs can give a text a commanding or instructive tone.

Ideas for starters and plenaries

- Ask students to suggest as many forms of non-fiction texts as they can and list their ideas on the whiteboard. Discuss which forms are likely to come up in the exam, using page 16 of this Teacher's Guide and underline them in the list. Add any types of text that students did not identify. Turn to page 16 in the Student Book and look at the list of source texts (numbered 7–13) on this page. Students should try to identify what types of texts these extracts belong to. They should be prepared to give reasons for their answers.

- Explain what is meant by 'audience', 'purpose' and 'form' and why it is important to try to identify these when analysing texts. Direct students to the source texts numbered 1–6 on pages 12 to 15 of the Student Book. For each text, students should make notes about intended audience, purpose and chosen form. Ask students to share their ideas with the class, giving reasons for their choices. Then, display Presentation 1.1.2, which gives more information about each text – does this information reflect what students have said about the texts?

- Ask students to look at the 'Health Challenge Wales' article on page 14 of the Student Book, which has been written to advise readers on how to lead a healthier lifestyle. Ask students to read the article and identify four ways that readers can improve their health, according to the text.

- For a more stretching task, provide students with copies of Activity Sheet 1.1.1, which includes an advert for days out at Legoland adventure park. Ask students to work in pairs to identify ten attractions that visitors can expect to find at the park, according to the text. Two example responses to this question are provided in Presentation 1.1.1.

- Discuss the differences between 'formal' and 'informal' language. Ask students to scan the source texts in Chapter 1.1 of the Student Book to find examples of formal and informal phrases. Alternatively, students can attempt Interactive 1.1.3, where they have to match each formal phrase to an informal version of the same phrase. How is a reader likely to react to formal language? How is a reader likely to react to informal language? Will the reader's reaction to this depend on other factors? Why might a writer opt to use formal or informal language to produce a piece of writing?

Lesson ideas

● Discuss what is meant by 'tone' in relation to written texts. Students could use Interactive 1.1.5 to practise identifying different types of tone. What features of writing contribute to tone? Encourage students to think about vocabulary, forms of address, variation of sentence lengths, level of detail, humour and use of rhetoric. Ask them to look at Extract 1 and Extract 2 on pages 12–13 of the Student Book. Working in pairs, students should produce a brief summary of the use of tone in each extract. What effect is this likely to have on the reader in each case? Students should then look at Extract 4 and Extract 5 on page 14 of the Student Book and work independently to complete the activity at the top of the page.

● Explain that selecting the right tone to suit the purpose and audience of a text is one way of making a text more persuasive. What other methods can writers use to persuade their readers to do something or adopt a particular point of view? Prompt students to think about choice of content; for example selecting information that best supports a particular opinion; using statistics or quotes from third parties; structuring information logically and providing counter-arguments. Divide students into small groups and ask each group to look at one of the source texts from Chapter 1.1 of the Student Book. In their groups, students should discuss what each text is trying to persuade the reader to do or think. What methods does the writer use to persuade the reader to do or think this? Ask each group to feed back to the class.

● Highlight the importance of backing-up points with specific evidence from the text. This evidence can be embedded into writing in the form or one-word quotations, or longer quotes. One-word quotations are particularly effective when closely considering vocabulary choices. Explain that students can list one-word examples, in order to build an effective picture of the patterns of language used in the text they are analysing. To practise this technique, ask students to work through some or all of the source texts in Chapter 1.1 of the Student Book. For each extract, ask students to pick out a group of words that illustrates something about the overall purpose and effect of the text. For example, in the case of the source text entitled 'Steer Clear of Car Crime' on page 12, students might pick out 'outsmart', 'simple steps' and 'secure', which are all examples of positive language that help to affirm the impression that people can successfully prevent crime.

● When carrying out a close reading of a text, students should think about how the writer has chosen to structure the text, both in terms of sentence types and choice of paragraphs. Ask Students to look at Extracts 7–13 provided on page 16 of the Student Book. In pairs, students should put together a comment for each text about how each writer uses sentences for effect. They should try to consider factors such as sentence length, sentence type and the combination of sentences in each text. Interactive 1.1.6 provides support for this exercise in the form of a matching activity, where students have to link annotations to appropriate examples.

● Having worked through and analysed sentence choices in short examples, ask students to apply what they have learned to a longer text from the Student Book, such as 'S.O.S Save our Stanley' on pages 20–21 or 'Manchester City are making a mockery of the game' on page 22. When working with longer texts, explain that it is not practical to comment on every single sentence. Students should comment on examples that are particularly revealing or striking and they should always ensure that the points they make are relevant to the question. In order to practise effective selection, limit the number of comments required for this activity to five points per text.

● Make the point that non-fiction texts often include features such as headings, sub-headings, varied fonts, colours, images and logos. These features can be analysed and commented on in the exam. Ask students to look at the texts numbered 1–6 on pages 12 to 15 of the Student Book and consider the headline used in each case. What does each headline suggest about the content of each text? What impact is each headline likely to have on the reader? Students should consider the tone, vocabulary, presentation, the formality/informality of the headline as well as how it connects to the rest of the text.

- Ask students to look at the section headed 'Comparing texts' on page 17 of the Student Book. Ask one student to read Text 14 to the class and ask another student to read Text 15 to the class. Ask the class to offer suggestions about what the intended audience might be for each text, and what the intended purpose is. Also, ask for suggestions about where readers might find each type of text. For example; would they be likely to appear in a holiday brochure, on an Internet review site, or on a letters page in a newspaper?

- Futher practice with identifying similarities and differences between texts and using comparitive language can be gained from Interactive 1.1.4, which includes two articles about dog owners. Use Interactive 1.1.1 to help students engage with Text 14 and Text 15. This activity is a quiz, which requires students to read each text carefully and pick out details that could be used as part of a comparison. This could be used in conjunction with the task that appears at the bottom of page 17 in the Student Book.

- Provide each student with a copy of Activity Sheet 1.1.2, which contains two short articles that deal with the subject matter of mineral water. Ask students to offer ideas about how they might compare and contrast these texts. List their ideas on the whiteboard and then discuss how to organize the best ones into a well-structured comparative response. Three example pieces of comparative writing are provided in Activity Sheet 1.1.3, which students could review – identifying the strengths and weaknesses of each piece.

A-A* students should...

- be able to select material appropriate to purpose and make valid comments and inferences based on the texts they read
- be able to respond to the detail as well as an overview of the text
- develop and sustain an interpretation of the writer's ideas and perspectives, selecting relevant points and explaining them with a clear depth of understanding
- successfully analyse the linguistic, grammatical, structural and presentational techniques used by each writer to create particular effects
- be able to compare texts effectively, offering coherent and perceptive comments and range confidently across both texts.

C-B students should...

- be able to select material appropriate to purpose and make valid comments and inferences based on the texts they read
- develop an interpretation of the writer's ideas and perspectives, selecting relevant points and explaining most of them with some depth of understanding
- analyse the linguistic, grammatical, structural and presentational techniques used by each writer and begin to address the question of 'how' each writer achieves particular effects
- show competence when comparing texts, making some valid cross-references and organizing points well.

E-D students should...

- be able to select material appropriate to purpose and make simple comments on surface features of the text
- show some awareness of the more obvious implicit meanings of the text
- make appropriate points about the writer's ideas and perspectives with some comment
- offer some comment on the linguistic, grammatical, structural and presentational techniques used by each writer with reference to the text
- make clear, if obvious, comparisons and contrasts between the texts.

Chapter 1.1b Non-Fiction Texts
How to teach GCSE English Unit 1

AO2

- Read and understand texts, selecting material appropriate to purpose, collating from different sources and making comparisons and cross-references as appropriate.
- Develop and sustain interpretations of writers' ideas and perspectives.
- Explain and evaluate how writers use linguistic, grammatical, structural and presentational features to achieve effects and engage and influence the reader.
- Understand texts in their social, cultural and historical contexts.

Introduction to the exam

Unit 1 will be assessed by an exam lasting one hour. Students will be provided with two non-fiction texts and will be asked to answer four questions on them. Some of these questions will ask students to focus on the first text and some of them will ask students to focus on the second text. The fourth question will ask students to compare and contrast both texts.

The non-fiction texts may include fact-sheets, leaflets or letters; or extracts from autobiographies, diaries, advertisements, reports, articles, webpages and brochures. The material will always include visual elements such as images, diagrams or the use of particular layout features.

There will be separate Foundation and Higher tier papers.

Example exam questions

All questions will test reading for understanding and meaning. Some questions will require students to read each source text and pick out relevant information. Higher tier questions may be worded as follows:

- According to this article, why/what/who/when…
- According to the writer of this letter, what/why/who/when…
- What is the writer's opinion of…
- What are the writer's thoughts about…

Foundation tier questions may provide additional support, such as suggesting how many points the student should aim to make in his or her answer. These questions may be worded as follows:

- List **ten**… mentioned in the brochure that are…
- List **three**… that take place in…
- List **four** of the facilities available in…
- List **ten** reasons given in the article for…

On Foundation and Higher tier papers, one question will ask students to focus on 'How' the writer of one of the texts achieves a particular effect. The effect stated in the question might be to interest, persuade, instruct or advise the reader. These questions may be worded as follows:

- How does the writer try to make his/her website/article interesting for his/her readers?
- How does the brochure/website persuade readers that…?
- How does the writer reveal the…?

- The writer of the article/letter/website/advertisement tries to... how does he/she do this?

For both papers, Question 4 will test the student's ability to compare both source texts. Questions may be presented as follows:

- Compare and contrast what... and... say about...
- Both of these texts are about... compare and contrast the texts.

Question 4 may also include a short bullet-point list of prompts suggesting what students should focus on in their answer.

Key ideas

- Different reading skills required:
  - location and reorganization – finding and rewording information
  - inference – reading 'between the lines'
  - appreciation of style – the way the author writes.
- When reading it is important to firstly identify the audience, purpose and format of the text.

- Things to think about when considering the voice of the text:
  - texts that use direct address, speak directly to the reader
  - texts can be written in a formal or informal tone
  - imperative verbs can give a text a commanding or instructive tone.

Ideas for starters and plenaries

- Ask students to suggest as many forms of non-fiction texts as they can and list their ideas on the whiteboard. Discuss which forms are likely to come up in the exam, using page 16 of this Teacher's Guide and underline them in the list. Add any types of text that students did not identify. Turn to page 16 in the Student Book and look at the list of source texts (numbered 7–13) on this page. Students should try to identify what types of texts these extracts belong to. They should be prepared to give reasons for their answers.

- Explain what is meant by 'audience', 'purpose' and 'form' and why it is important to try to identify these when analysing texts. Direct students to the source texts numbered 1–6 on pages 12 to 15 of the Student Book. For each text, students should make notes about intended audience, purpose and chosen form. Encourage students to share some of their ideas with the class, giving reasons for their choices. Then, display Presentation 1.1.2, which gives more information about each text – does this information reflect what students have said about the texts?

- Ask students to look at the text entitled 'How Jamie Saved Me' on page 19 of the Student Book, which is a web article about Jamie Oliver. Ask students to read the article and identify five positive comments that the writer makes about the chef.

- For a more stretching task, provide students with copies of Activity Sheet 1.1.1, which includes an advert for days out at Legoland adventure park. Ask students to work in pairs to identify ten attractions that visitors can expect to find at the park, according to the text. Two example responses to this question are provided in Presentation 1.1.1.

- Discuss the differences between 'formal' and 'informal' language. Ask students to scan the source texts in Chapter 1.1 of the Student Book to find examples of formal and informal phrases. Alternatively, students can attempt Interactive 1.1.3, where they have to match each formal phrase to an informal version of the same phrase. How is a reader likely to react to formal language? How is a reader likely to react to informal language? Is the reader's reaction likely to depend on other factors? Why might a writer opt to use formal or informal language to produce a piece of writing?

Lesson ideas

- Discuss what is meant by 'tone' in relation to written texts. Students could use Interactive 1.1.5 to practise identifying different types of tone. What features of writing contribute to tone? Encourage students to think about vocabulary, forms of address, variation of sentence lengths, level of detail, humour and use of rhetoric. Ask them to look at Extract 1 and Extract 2 on pages 12–13 of the Student Book. Working in pairs, students should produce a brief summary of the use of tone in each extract. What effect is this likely to have on the reader in each case? Students should then look at Extract 4 and Extract 5 on page 14 of the Student Book and work independently to complete the activity at the top of the page.

- Explain that selecting the right tone to suit the purpose and audience of a text is one way of making a text more persuasive. What other methods can writers use to persuade their readers to do something or adopt a particular point of view? Prompt students to think about choice of content; for example selecting information that best supports a particular opinion; using statistics or quotes from third parties; structuring information logically and providing counter-arguments. Divide students into small groups and ask each group to look at one of the source texts from Chapter 1.1 of the Student Book. In their groups, students should discuss what each text is trying to persuade the reader to do or think. What methods does the writer use to persuade the reader to do or think this? Ask each group to feed back to the class.

- Highlight the importance of backing-up points with specific evidence from the text. This evidence can be embedded into writing in the form or one-word quotations, or longer quotes. One-word quotations are particularly effective when closely considering vocabulary choices. Explain that students can list one-word examples, in order to build an effective picture of the patterns of language used in the text they are analysing. To practise this technique, ask students to work through some or all of the source texts in Chapter 1.1 of the Student Book. For each extract, ask students to pick out a group of words that illustrates something about the overall purpose and effect of the text. For example, in the case of the source text entitled 'Steer Clear of Car Crime' on page 12, students might pick out 'outsmart', 'simple steps' and 'secure', which are all examples of positive language that help to affirm the impression that people can successfully prevent crime.

- When carrying out a close reading of a text, students should think about how the writer has chosen to structure the text, both in terms of sentence types and choice of paragraphs. Ask Students to look at Extracts 7–13 provided on page 16 of the Student Book. In pairs, students should put together a comment for each text about how each writer uses sentences for effect. They should try to consider factors such as sentence length, sentence type and the combination of sentences in each text. Interactive 1.1.6 provides support for this exercise in the form of a matching activity, where students have to link annotations to appropriate examples.

- Having worked through and analysed sentence choices in short examples, ask students to apply what they have learned to a longer text from the Student Book, such as 'S.O.S Save our Stanley' on pages 20–21 or 'Manchester City are making a mockery of the game' on page 22. When working with longer texts, explain that it is not practical to comment on every single sentence. Students should comment on examples that are particularly revealing or striking and they should always ensure that the points they make are relevant to the question. In order to practise effective selection, limit the number of comments required for this activity to five points per text.

- Make the point that non-fiction texts often include features such as headings, sub-headings, varied fonts, colours, images and logos. These features can be analysed and commented on in the exam. Ask students to look at the texts numbered 1–6 on pages 12 to 15 of the Student Book and consider the headline used in each case. What does each headline suggest about the content of each text? What impact is each headline likely to have on the reader? Students should consider the tone, vocabulary, presentation, the formality/informality of the headline as well as how it connects to the rest of the text.

- Ask students to look at the two articles on whaling on page 18 of the Student Book. Ask one student to read Text 16 to the class and ask another student to read Text 17 to the class. Ask students to offer suggestions about what the intended audience might be for each text, and what the intended purpose is. Also, ask for suggestions about where readers might find each type of text. For example; would they be likely to appear in a leaflet from a charity organization, on a travel website or as part of a magazine feature?

- Further practice with identifying similarities and differences between texts and using comparative language can be gained from Interactive 1.1.4, which includes two articles about dog owners. Use Interactive 1.1.2 to help students engage with Text 16 and Text 17. This activity is a quiz, which requires students to read each text and pick out details that could be used as part of a comparison. This could be used in conjunction with the task that appears at the bottom of page 18 in the Student Book.

- Provide each student with a copy of Activity Sheet 1.1.2, which contains two short articles that deal with the subject matter of mineral water. Ask students to offer ideas about how they might compare and contrast these texts. List their ideas on the whiteboard and then discuss how to organize the best ones into a well-structured comparative response. Three example pieces of comparative writing are provided in Activity Sheet 1.1.3, which students could review – identifying the strengths and weaknesses of each piece.

A-A* students should...

- be able to select material appropriate to purpose and make valid comments and inferences based on the texts they read
- be able to respond to the detail as well as an overview of the text
- develop and sustain an interpretation of the writer's ideas and perspectives, selecting relevant points and explaining them with a clear depth of understanding
- successfully analyse the linguistic, grammatical, structural and presentational techniques used by each writer to create particular effects
- be able to compare texts effectively, offering coherent and perceptive comments and range confidently across both texts.

C-B students should...

- be able to select material appropriate to purpose and make valid comments and inferences based on the texts they read
- develop an interpretation of the writer's ideas and perspectives, selecting relevant points and explaining most of them with some depth of understanding
- analyse the linguistic, grammatical, structural and presentational techniques used by each writer and begin to address the question of 'how' each writer achieves particular effects
- show competence when comparing texts, making some valid cross-references and organizing points well.

D-E students should...

- be able to select material appropriate to purpose and make simple comments on surface features of the text
- show some awareness of the more obvious implicit meanings of the text
- make appropriate points about the writer's ideas and perspectives with some comment
- offer some comment on the linguistic, grammatical, structural and presentational techniques used by each writer with reference to the text
- make clear, if obvious, comparisons and contrasts between the texts.

Chapter 1.2 Contemporary Poetry
How to teach GCSE English Literature Unit 1 Section B

AO1
- Respond to texts critically and imaginatively; select and evaluate relevant textual detail to illustrate and support interpretations.

AO2
- Explain how language, structure and form contribute to writers' presentation of ideas, themes and settings.

AO3
- Make comparisons and explain links between texts, evaluating writers' different ways of expressing meaning and achieving effects.

Introduction to the exam

Unit 1 will be tested by a two-hour exam. Students are advised to spend one hour on Section B, which will require them to answer a question comparing two unseen contemporary poems. The question will include a list of bullet-point prompts to help students structure their answers. There will be separate exam papers for Foundation and Higher tiers.

Example exam questions

Students will be required to answer one question for Unit 1 Section B. The question will include two unseen poems and a list of prompts suggesting what students should focus on in their answers. The question will also provide one or two lines to contextualize each text. The task may be presented as follows:

In the first of the following poems… In the second…

Write about both poems and their effect on you. Show how they are similar and how they are different.

You may write about each poem separately and then compare them, or make comparisons where appropriate in your answer as a whole.

You may wish to include some or all of these points:
- *the content of the poems – what they are about;*
- *the ideas the poets may have wanted us to think about;*
- *the mood or atmosphere of the poems;*
- *how they are written – words and phrases you find interesting, the way they are organized, and so on;*
- *your responses to the poems.*

Key ideas

- Break-down of the requirements of the task:
  - unseen – responding to a poem that has not been studied before
  - poetry – read for meaning, sentence by sentence
  - comparison – making connections between two poems.
- Annotations should be short and written in note-form; they can be written directly on to the question paper as a means of generating initial ideas.
- Identifying the voice and situation are key starting points for understanding a poem.
- An 'image' in writing is a picture created in the mind of the reader.

- Images can be literal (descriptive) or non-literal (figurative).
- Figurative images include:
  - similes – indirect comparison using 'as' or 'like'
  - metaphors – direct comparison using 'is/was'.
- Things to consider when writing about poetry:
  - content
  - ideas
  - mood and atmosphere
  - how the poem is written
  - providing a personal response
  - how the first poem is similar to/different from the second poem.

Ideas for starters and plenaries

- Before students come into the classroom, place a copy of two linked, unseen poems face-down on each desk. You could use copies of poems from the Student Book, which are all included on the OxBox in printable form. Put an example exam question on the board, or provide a series of related questions designed to guide students through a full exam question. Presentation 1.2.4 includes a customizable question that is based on the format of the exam. When students come in, tell them to look at the poem on their desk and the question on the board. Explain that in their exam for this unit, they will have to express their views on two unseen poems and respond to the kind of the question/s displayed on the board. What do they find most challenging or daunting about this task? What skills or knowledge would make the task easier? What would they need to establish first before attempting to write a response?

- Explain the importance of identifying the 'voice' and 'situation' of a poem before studying it in close detail. Explain that 'voice' refers literally to the voice that speaks in the poem and its perspective and that 'situation' refers to what happens, including where the poem is set, when it is set, who it in involves and what it focuses on. Present extracts from unseen poems on the board and read them aloud. What observations are students able to make about voice and situation in regards to the extracts? How did they draw these conclusions? Build a list of suggestions and techniques on the board.

- Read the poem entitled 'Hurricane' on page 39 of the Student Book. Taking each stanza in turn, ask students to suggest what the mood or atmosphere is in the stanza and then ask a student to re-read this stanza emphasizing this mood by selecting an appropriate tone of voice, stressing key words and using punctuation to dramatic effect. Once the whole poem has been read in this way, identify and discuss any key moments in the poem where the mood shifts or changes. What is the impact of this change? The same activity could be carried out for 'Autumn' on page 40 of the Student Book.

- Ask students to write three examples of their own 'literal' poetic images and three examples of 'figurative' images. They could refer to the definitions on page 42 of the Student Book for guidance. Figurative images can either be presented in the form of a metaphor or a simile. Ask students to read out some of their images to the class. After a number of examples have been collected, ask for feedback from the class. Do any images stick in the mind? Why is this? Were some particularly striking or particularly unconvincing? Discuss what makes certain imagery effective and why writers build imagery into their poetry.

Lesson ideas

- Discuss concepts associated with poetry with the class to establish what is understood by the words: content, ideas, mood/atmosphere, language and personal response. Students can attempt a matching exercise in Interactive 1.2.1 to consolidate their understanding of these terms.

- Ask students to read 'Hurricane' by James Berry on page 39 of the Student Book. A printable version of this poem is provided on the OxBox (Activity Sheet 1.2.3), which students can annotate. Ask students to work in small groups to answer the questions on page 41 and page 42 of the Student Book. They could use Activity Sheet 1.2.4 to record their thoughts.

- Then ask students to approach 'Autumn' by Alan Bold in a similar way. This poem appears on page 40 of the Student Book and a printable version of this poem is included on the OxBox (Activity Sheet 1.2.6). In their groups, students should answer the questions on pages 42 and 43, paying close attention to where these questions prompt them to refer back to 'Hurricane' in order to make comparisons. Students could use Activity Sheet 1.2.5 to record their responses.

- Look at the poems 'Morning' and 'In Praise of the Great Bull Walrus' on pages 45 and 46 of the Student Book. Ask students to read each poem. What is each poem about? What can be said about the voice in each poem? Students could consider the tone, perspective, attitude and focus of the voice. Students could attempt the activities on pages 47 and 48, firstly concentrating on 'Morning' and then looking at the second poem. They could use copies of Activity Sheet 1.2.7 to record their thoughts.

- Having responded to the questions on pages 47–48 of the Student Book, ask students to read the student answer on pages 49 and 50. For each paragraph ask students to note down one thing that works well and one thing that could be developed or improved. Their points could relate to the content or the written style of the essay. A printable version of this student response is provided on the OxBox (Activity Sheet 1.2.8), which students can use to annotate. This might be useful if you would like students to carry out this activity without referring to the Examiner's comment on page 50. If students do refer to the Examiner's comment for ideas, you could make the task more challenging by asking students to assess each paragraph of the response on its own merits and provide more detailed feedback about what this student could do to improve on the points the examiner mentions.

- The OxBox provides further texts and further support for approaching comparative writing tasks. Activity Sheet 1.2.1 includes a copy of 'The Concerned Adolescent' by Wendy Cope. Read the poem to the class. Using Presentation 1.2.1, ask students to answer questions on this unseen text. The questions could be attempted in small groups or as a class. Then ask students to carry out the same activity for a second poem: 'Stopping Places' by Molly Holden. Use Activity Sheet 1.2.2 and Presentation 1.2.2 for this.

- Discuss with students how they might go about comparing 'The Concerned Adolescent' by Wendy Cope and 'Stopping Places' by Molly Holden, based on the ideas they have generated in response to the questions they have already answered. Display Presentation 1.2.3 for guidance.

- Set up students to attempt the practice exam paper set-out on pages 51 and 52 of the Student Book under exam conditions. Allow students 1 hour to complete the task. To avoid students basing their answer on the sample response that begins on page 53, it might work better to provide them with a photocopy of the sample paper and collect in the Student Books. Alternatively, this practice paper is included on the OxBox and can be printed out and given to students. Collect the responses in at the end of the lesson. At the beginning of the next lesson, hand the responses out to students and ask them to assess their work against the checklists provided on page 53 of the Student Book. Ask students to read the high-band sample response on pages 53 and 54. How does this compare to their work? Did this writer identify any different points? What did this writer do better? What did the student feel he or she did better than this writer? Ask students to feed some of their ideas back to the class. Remind students that there is no such thing as a 'right' answer when writing about poetry. It is important to offer a personal response to the poems and original thinking will be rewarded by examiners.

A-A* students should...

- respond confidently to texts and convey their ideas clearly and persuasively, backing up their points with well-selected quotations
- show appreciation of how writers use language, structure and form to achieve specific effects, including the use of stylistic features
- maintain a sustained discussion of the links and comparisons between texts and make effective cross-references
- identify subtle points of comparison as well as more obvious ones and probe links confidently
- write a clear and fluent response that is well-structured, with few errors in grammar, punctuation and spelling
- use specialist vocabulary effectively.

C-B students should...

- respond to the text with increasing confidence, explaining points thoroughly and making detailed reference to the text
- demonstrate how writers use ideas, themes and settings to affect the reader
- show increasing appreciation of how language, structure and form are combined to convey meanings and ideas
- make relevant comparisons between texts, identifying links in terms of subject, theme and style
- produce a response that is relatively clear and fluent, with a good structure and only minor errors in spelling and punctuation
- make appropriate use of specialist vocabulary.

D-E students should...

- show some understanding of the main features of the text and make reference to relevant points through echoing and paraphrasing
- recognize and comment on features of style and structure in brief or simple terms
- make straightforward links and comparisons between texts, identifying obvious features of similarity and difference
- produce a response, which is reasonably clear and structured, with most simple words spelt correctly
- make some use of specialist vocabulary.

Chapter 1.3a Literary Heritage Poetry and Shakespeare
How to teach GCSE English Unit 3 Section A

AO2

- Read and understand texts, selecting material appropriate to purpose, collating from different sources and making comparisons and cross-references as appropriate.
- Develop and sustain interpretations of writers' ideas and perspectives.
- Explain and evaluate how writers use linguistic, grammatical, structural and presentational features to achieve effects and engage and influence the reader.
- Understand texts in their social, cultural and historical contexts.

Introduction to the Controlled Assessment

Unit 3 will be tested by Controlled Assessment. Students will be required to submit two assignments, the first of which will ask students to link a Shakespeare play that they have studied to a range of literary heritage poems from the WJEC poetry collection. The poems and the play will be related thematically.

Tasks will be set by WJEC every year and WJEC will release a suggested list of poems for study in April in the year before candidates are entered for this unit and at the same time as the release of the tasks. These tasks may be contextualized. Unlike the examined units, there is no split between Foundation and Higher tiers.

During the research and planning stage students may use reference materials and may seek general advice from teachers. They may also work with other students. They must not, however, produce a draft of their final response.

The final assignment must be completed under controlled conditions within four hours. Students will be able to take clean copies of the texts they have studied into the final assessment with them, along with one A4 sheet of notes prepared in advance. This sheet of notes should not include a pre-prepared draft or an outline of the response. When completing their final assignment, students must work individually and must not have access to tools such as dictionaries, thesauri or reference materials. This also applies if they are completing their work on a computer. Centres must therefore ensure that students cannot use spell checks or grammar checks and cannot access the Internet.

The final assessment can be divided up into shorter sessions. If this is the case, work must be collected in at the end of each session and locked away securely until the beginning of the next. Once work is submitted for assessment at the end of the last session, students may not revise it.

The second assignment for this part of the unit will require students to study a different cultures prose text. This is covered in more detail in Chapter 1.4b of this Teacher's Guide.

Example reading tasks

Tasks may be presented as generic tasks that can be applied to whatever text the student has studied or they may be specific, relating to particular texts. The question below is an example of a generic task:

> In order to complete this task you will need to have read a play by Shakespeare and the following poems from the WJEC poetry collection:
>
> *Porphyria's Lover, Human Interest, To His Coy Mistress, Sonnet 130, The Beggar Woman, Song: The Willing Mistriss, Twice Shy, They Did Not Expect This, Meeting Point, Whoso List to Hunt, A Married State, Song of the Worker's Wife, Afternoons, A Woman to her Lover, Sonnet 116, Havisham.*
>
> Many plays and poems are concerned with the relationship between men and women. Choose one relationship between a man and a woman in the drama you have studied and compare it with a similar relationship in the poetry you have studied.

Specific tasks may be presented as follows:

> How does Shakespeare portray the theme of grief in *King Lear* throughout the play?
>
> The theme also features in a number of the poems you have studied. Discuss how the emotion of grief is portrayed in the poetry you have studied.
>
> What is your personal response to the literature you have studied? In your answer you must explore the links between the poetry and the Shakespeare play.

> Look at the way Shakespeare presents Juliet's relationship with her parents in *Romeo & Juliet*. Consider what her parents think about how women should behave and Juliet's reaction to their views.
>
> Consider how the role of women is presented in poems in the collection. Write about one poem in particular but make references to others.
>
> What is your personal response to the literature you have studied? In your answer you must explore the links between the poetry and the Shakespeare play.

Key ideas

Literary heritage poetry

- Opening lines of poetry – establish the voice and situation of the poem early on.
- Literary heritage poetry can be divided into two periods – poetry written before the First World War (pre-1914) and poetry written after the war (post-1914 poetry).
- Identifying themes in poetry:
  - love
  - family and parent-child relationships
  - youth and age
  - power and ambition
  - male-female relationships and the role of women
  - hypocrisy and prejudice
  - conflict
  - grief.
- Tips for studying poetry:
  - identify who is speaking in the poem
  - work out what the situation is in the poem early on
  - read the poem sentence-by-sentence
  - try to hear the words of the poem as you read

Key ideas (continued...)

- ◆ poems may refer to people, places, events and have twisting plots so be prepared to comment on them
  - ◆ remember there is often no 'right' answer when responding to poetry.
- Questions to ask when reading poetry:
  - ◆ What is the poem about?
  - ◆ From whose point of view is the poem written?
  - ◆ What is the mood/atmosphere of the poem?
  - ◆ How is the poem written?
  - ◆ What is your personal response to the poem?
- Analysing the writer's choice of words and phrases:
  - ◆ What stands out?
  - ◆ What is especially effective/surprising?
  - ◆ Are there any subtle/suggested meanings?
  - ◆ Which words have a strong impact?
  - ◆ What images are created?
  - ◆ Do the words involve the senses?
  - ◆ How do the words affect the mood/atmosphere of the poem?
  - ◆ Does the language create any contrasts or tension in the poem?
- Analysing the writer's choice of structure:
  - ◆ What stands out?
  - ◆ Are there any features that confuse/clarify the meaning?
  - ◆ Are there any interesting sound patterns in the poem?
- Technical terms are only useful where they can be used to explain and analyse relevant features of the poem and their effects on the reader.
- Biographical details and cultural contexts:
  - ◆ biographical details – relevant facts about a poet's life
  - ◆ cultural contexts – relevant details about the historical periods and locations that relate to the poem
  - ◆ where included, facts should always be related to the main points of the response
  - ◆ contextual information should be woven into the response, not added on as a separate section of writing.

Shakespeare

- Shakespeare's tragedies often end with the deaths of major characters.
- Shakespeare's comedies often end with marriages and celebrations.

- Tragedies might include comic elements and equally, comedies can sometimes deal with darker issues.
- Other types of Shakespearean plays include:
  - ◆ problem plays – feature elements of both comedies and tragedies but also deal with serious moral issues, e.g. *The Merchant of Venice* and *Measure for Measure*
  - ◆ romances – have happy endings like comedies but also feature magical elements, e.g. *The Tempest* and *The Winter's Tale*
  - ◆ history plays – based on famous figures or episodes from history, e.g. *Henry V, Richard III.*
- Tips for reading Shakespeare:
  - ◆ read the list of characters before reading the play and be aware of who the characters are
  - ◆ pronounce individual words
  - ◆ read slowly and deliberately
  - ◆ use the punctuation
  - ◆ identify the difference between verse and prose
  - ◆ take note of entrances and exits to keep track of who is on stage
  - ◆ pay attention to stage directions
  - ◆ distinguish between speech that takes place between characters and speech that takes place between a character and the audience in an aside or soliloquy.
- Shakespeare's verse is usually unrhymed, with rhyming lines used for emphasis or at the end of key speeches.
- Characters are usually able to switch between speaking in prose or verse depending on who they are talking to and why.
- Prose could be used for speech that is informal, secretive, disrespectful, heart-felt, despairing or fearful – a whole host of subtle emotions.

Comparison

- Possible points of comparison between texts:
  - ◆ key themes
  - ◆ personal response
  - ◆ mood
  - ◆ viewpoint
  - ◆ narrative
  - ◆ setting
  - ◆ type
  - ◆ structure
  - ◆ style
  - ◆ period.

Ideas for starters and plenaries

- Write the title and first line of each poem from the WJEC Literary Heritage Poetry Collection on a small piece of paper and put these into a hat. Students must pick a poem from the hat and then attempt to write the second line. This is a creative exercise rather than a memory test, so students should try to engage with the opening line and create a suitable continuation that is both relevant to the subject matter and in keeping with the poet's style of writing. You could print out a copy of Activity Sheet 1.3.10 to use for this, which includes the titles and first lines of all poems in the collection. Ask students to read out some of their creations and compare these to the actual poems. Discuss the meanings intended by students when writing their versions and the meaning conveyed through the actual versions from the collection.

- Prompt students to draw on their existing knowledge of Shakespeare by working in groups to create a spider diagram containing facts, opinions and contextual references. Divide students into groups of three or four and give each group a sheet of A3 paper. You could prompt students to consider topics such as: why Shakespeare is still studied in schools, best Shakespeare film adaptations, favourite Shakespeare characters, facts about Elizabethan life, biographical facts about Shakespeare and relevant technical terms such as soliloquy, dramatic irony, iambic pentameter, rhyming couplets, tragedy and comedy. Ask students to feed back their ideas to the class. You could also attempt Interactive 1.3.1 as a class, which provides a quiz based on Chapter 1.3 of the Student Book.

- Take each scene in turn from the play that students are studying and pick a group of students to perform the entrances and exits from the scene in front of the class. The stage directions should be read out so that the rest of the class can identify who is who. The 'actors' should perform these snapshots of the action from the play without speaking. They should use body language and distinguishing props or mannerisms to help the audience identify who each person is intended to represent. Activity Sheet 1.3.6 provides further support for this activity and examples from *Twelfth Night*.

- Working in small groups, students should come up with a newspaper-style headline for each scene of the play they are studying. In order to devise a headline that is suitably attention-grabbing, they should consider what the most dramatic events are in the scene. Activity Sheet 1.3.7 provides a template for presenting each headline.

- Ask students to take it in turns to read aloud from 'The Seven Ages of Man' by Shakespeare on page 78 of the Student Book paying close attention to the punctuation. The punctuation has been highlighted in orange in this text so that it stands out. Students should refer to the 'Reading the text' section on page 77 of the Student Book for tips on how to read Shakespeare.

Lesson ideas

- Discuss the format of the Controlled Assessment using the question and answer material headed 'The Writing Process' on page 89 of the Student Book as a starting point. Presentation 1.3.11 provides additional support for approaching the types of tasks that students are likely to undertake for their assessment. Ask students to then look at the sample tasks provided in Chapter 1.3 of the Student Book. Discuss what each question is asking students to do in each case and what they should aim to cover if they were planning a response to it. Electronic versions of all the sample tasks are provided on the OxBox, so they can be easily displayed and annotated on an interactive whiteboard. The example tasks provided in this chapter of the Teacher's Guide are also available in electronic format in Activity Sheet 1.3.11, which can be displayed or given to students.

- To get students thinking about themes, write one of the eight themes from this unit on the whiteboard, chosen from the following list: love; family and parent-child relationships; youth and age; power and ambition; male-female relationships and the role of women; hypocrisy and prejudice; conflict and grief. Alternatively, you could use Presentation 1.3.9, which includes a screen for each theme. Explain that different writers can approach the same theme from different perspectives – for example, from an optimistic, pessimistic or realistic point of view. For the theme you have displayed, ask students to suggest possible perspectives. Prompt them to provide a mixture of optimistic, pessimistic and rational viewpoints. For example: for 'youth and age', a pessimistic perspective could be: 'young people and old people never understand each other' or an optimistic perspective could be: 'young people can learn a lot from older people'. Consider other themes from the unit. Students could use Activity Sheet 1.3.3 to record their thoughts.

- Look at page 58 of the Student Book, which covers how to read the opening of a poem. Explain why it is important to establish the speaker and situation early on and how a good understanding of the opening lines of a poem can help the reader to develop a deeper insight into the overall text. Students can put this into practise by attempting the activities on pages 59–61 which focus on a number of poems from the WJEC GCSE Poetry Collection. They could use Activity Sheet 1.3.9 to record their thoughts.

- Ask students to look at the 'Themes and words' section on page 81 of the Student Book and the quotations from various Shakespeare plays, which appear on pages 82 to 84. For each quotation, ask students to identify which themes are relevant to it from the following list: love; family and parent-child relationships; youth and age; power and ambition; male-female relationships and the role of women; hypocrisy and prejudice; conflict and grief. You could display Presentation 1.3.8 on the whiteboard for reference, which lists all of these themes.

- What are the three most significant moments in the play in terms of plot development? Ask students to think about the entire plot of the play they are studying and select three events that are important in terms of character development, progress of the plot or dramatic impact. Ask students to feed back to the class and add their ideas to the whiteboard. Once a number of ideas have been collated, ask students to vote for the moments that they think are the most critical in terms of the plot and ask some of them to explain their choices. Highlight the top three events on the board.

- Referring again to pages 82 to 84 of the Student Book, select a number of the quotations at random and discuss the themes that students have identified. Ask them to comment on how the theme is dealt with in the quotation. What more can they say about the theme and how it is presented?

- Select an extract from the play that students are studying for this unit and display Presentation 1.3.3. Ask students to work in pairs to answer the questions relating to themes. Students should discuss the questions in their pairs and make notes before feeding back to the class with their ideas. A question sheet is also provided for relationships (Presentation 1.3.4), allowing students to carry out the same activity with a different focus.

- Pick a theme from the list of themes that relate to this unit (love; family and parent-child relationships; youth and age; power and ambition; male-female relationships and the role of women; hypocrisy and prejudice; conflict and grief). Ask students to work in pairs to select five significant quotations from the play they are studying that reveal something about this theme in the play. You could ask the whole class to work with the same theme, or you could ask different pairs to work with different themes and then feedback to the class. Students could use Activity Sheet 1.3.8 to record their thoughts.

- How is the experience of watching a play different to reading a poem or a novel? Ask students to suggest as many ideas as they can think of and write them on the board. Highlight answers such as: the audience actually sees a play and hears the words that the characters speak; the audience experiences the play with other members of the audience; stage directions are acted out; the performance might include sound effects, music or special effects; different performances of the same play may be different because they depend on the decisions of the director; the pace of the performance is determined by the director and the actors rather than the reader.

- Explain that when reading a play, it is important to always think of it as a performance and be aware of how the words on the page might be spoken or acted out on stage. Ask students to look at the section headed 'Entrances and exits' on page 79 of the Student Book. Highlight the point that understanding the significance of a character's speech and actions at a given moment in the play depends upon knowledge of who else is on stage at the same time.

- Discuss the use of verse and prose in Shakespeare with reference to page 79 of the Student Book. Make the point that there are no strict rules associated with verse and prose and that the choice of form is always connected to the specific context of each speech or piece of dialogue. For example, who is speaking to who, what they are talking about, whether the speaker is happy, tense or angry. Students should consider these principles in light of the text they are studying by attempting the activities on page 79. Activity Sheet 1.3.5 provides further support for these activities.

- Referring to the play or plays that students are studying, ask them to make a list of all the soliloquies that appear in the play or in a particular act of a play they are focusing on. Explain that a soliloquy is a speech that is delivered directly to the audience, often when a character is alone on stage. Ask students to add one or two lines about what each speech is about. They could use copies of Activity Sheet 1.3.1 to record their notes. Select one or two speeches from those that students have identified and discuss with the class why the character delivers this alone on stage, or out of earshot of other characters. Discuss the dramatic impact of this.

A-A* students should...

- respond critically to the texts, identifying subtle links and telling comparisons between whole texts
- present points persuasively and select textual references carefully, commenting fully on significant words, phrases and stylistic features
- offer detailed and original interpretations of language patterns, stylistic features and the use of imagery across whole texts
- confidently evaluate and comment on character relationships, and characters' attitudes and motives
- demonstrate a clear understanding of the social, cultural and historical contexts that are relevant to the texts and identify the importance of these factors when interpreting them
- show an awareness of literary tradition and the ability to link details of a text to its literary background
- make relevant points about how texts have been, or continue to be, influential at different times.

C-B students should...

- respond critically to texts offering a personal response, referring to aspects of language, grammar and structure to support their views
- select and evaluate textual details confidently and appropriately, demonstrating how writers convey information and meaning through their texts
- compare texts successfully, making cross-references between texts
- convey their ideas clearly and appropriately
- identify appropriate contexts successfully and begin to show an awareness of how texts have been influential over time.

D-E students should...

- respond to the main ideas and themes of the texts
- make simple comparisons and cross-references between texts
- offer a personal response to the text and begin to select relevant and appropriate textual details to support their views
- demonstrate basic awareness of how writers achieve effects through specific language choices
- show some awareness of social/cultural and historical contexts that relate to the texts they have studied and begin to suggest how this is relevant to understanding the texts.

Chapter 1.3b Literary Heritage Poetry and Shakespeare

How to teach GCSE English Literature Unit 3

AO1

- Respond to texts critically and imaginatively; select and evaluate relevant textual detail to illustrate and support interpretations.

AO2

- Explain how language, structure and form contribute to writers' presentation of ideas, themes and settings.

AO3

- Make comparisons and explain links between texts, evaluating writers' different ways of expressing meaning and achieving effects.

Introduction to the Controlled Assessment

Unit 3 will be tested by Controlled Assessment. Students will be required to submit one assignment, where they must link a Shakespeare play to a range of literary heritage poems from the WJEC poetry collection. They may study any Shakespeare play except *Othello* and *Much Ado about Nothing*. The poems and the play will be related thematically.

WJEC will release a suggested list of poems for study in April in the year before candidates are entered for this unit and at the same time as the release of the tasks. Tasks will be set by WJEC every year. Unlike the examined units, the Controlled Assessment is untiered.

During the research and planning stage students may use reference materials and may seek general advice from teachers. They may also work with other students. They must not, however, produce a draft of their final response. The final assignment must be completed under controlled conditions within four hours. During this time students will be able to consult clean copies of the texts they have studied and one A4 sheet of their own notes prepared in advance. This sheet of notes should not include a pre-prepared draft or an outline of the response.

When completing their final assignment, students must work individually. The final assessment can be divided up into shorter sessions. If this is the case work must be collected in at the end of each session and locked away securely until the beginning of the next. Once work is submitted for assessment at the end of the last session, it may not be revised.

Example reading tasks

Tasks may be presented as generic tasks that can be applied to whatever text the student has studied or they may be specific, relating to particular texts. The following question is an example of a generic task:

> In order to complete this task you will need to have read a play by Shakespeare and the following poems from the WJEC poetry collection:
>
> *Porphyria's Lover, Human Interest, To His Coy Mistress, Sonnet 130, The Beggar Woman, Song: The Willing Mistriss, Twice Shy, They Did Not Expect This, Meeting Point, Whoso List to Hunt, A Married State, Song of the Worker's Wife, Afternoons, A Woman to Her Lover, Sonnet 160, Havisham.*
>
> Many plays and poems are concerned with the relationship between men and women. Choose one relationship between a man and a woman in the drama you have studied and compare it with a similar relationship in the poetry you have studied.

Specific tasks may be presented as follows:

> How does Shakespeare portray the theme of grief in King Lear throughout the play?
>
> The theme also features in a number of the poems you have studied. Discuss how the emotion of grief is portrayed in the poetry you have studied.
>
> What is your personal response to the literature you have studied? In your answer you must explore the links between the poetry and the Shakespeare play.

> Look at the way Shakespeare presents Juliet's relationship with her parents in *Romeo & Juliet*. Consider what her parents think about how women should behave and Juliet's reaction to their views.
>
> Consider how the role of women is presented in poems in the collection. Write about one poem in particular but make references to others.
>
> What is your personal response to the literature you have studied? In your answer you must explore the links between the poetry and the Shakespeare play.

Key ideas

Literary heritage poetry

- Opening lines of poetry – establish the voice and situation of the poem early on.
- Literary heritage poetry can be divided into two periods – poetry written before the First World War (pre-1914) and poetry written after the war (post-1914 poetry).
- Identifying themes in poetry:
  - love
  - family and parent-child relationships
  - youth and age
  - power and ambition
  - male-female relationships and the role of women
  - hypocrisy and prejudice
  - conflict
  - grief.
- Tips for studying poetry:
  - read the poem sentence-by-sentence
  - try to hear the words of the poem as you read

Key ideas (continued...)

- ◆ poems may refer to people, places, events and have twisting plots so be prepared to comment on them
- ◆ remember there is often no 'right' answer when responding to poetry.
- Questions to ask when reading poetry:
  - ◆ What is the poem about?
  - ◆ From whose point of view is the poem written?
  - ◆ What is the mood/atmosphere of the poem?
  - ◆ How is the poem written?
  - ◆ What is your personal response to the poem?
- Analysing the writer's choice of words and phrases:
  - ◆ What stands out?
  - ◆ What is especially effective/surprising?
  - ◆ Are there any subtle/suggested meanings?
  - ◆ Which words have a strong impact?
  - ◆ What images are created?
  - ◆ Do the words involve the senses?
  - ◆ How do the words affect the mood/ atmosphere of the poem?
  - ◆ Does the language create any contrasts or tensions in the poem?
- Analysing the writer's choice of structure:
  - ◆ What stands out?
  - ◆ Are there any features that confuse/clarify the meaning?
  - ◆ Are there any interesting sound patterns in the poem?
- Technical terms are only useful where they can be used to explain relevant features of the poem and the effects on the reader.
- Biographical details and cultural contexts:
  - ◆ biographical details – relevant facts about a poet's life
  - ◆ cultural contexts – relevant details about the historical periods and locations that relate to the poem
  - ◆ where included, facts should always be related to the main points of the response
  - ◆ contextual information should be woven into the response, not added on as a separate section of writing.

Shakespeare

- Shakespeare's tragedies often end with the deaths of major characters.
- Shakespeare's comedies often end with marriages and celebrations.

- Tragedies might include comic elements and equally, comedies can sometimes deal with darker issues.
- Other types of Shakespearean plays include:
  - ◆ problem plays – feature elements of both comedies and tragedies but also deal with serious, dramatic moral issues, e.g. *The Merchant of Venice* and *Measure for Measure*
  - ◆ romances – have happy endings like comedies but also feature magical elements, e.g. *The Tempest* and *The Winter's Tale*
  - ◆ history plays – based on famous figures or episodes from history, e.g. *Henry V, Richard III.*
- Tips for reading Shakespeare:
  - ◆ read the list of characters before reading the play and be aware of who the characters are
  - ◆ pronounce individual words
  - ◆ read slowly and deliberately
  - ◆ use the punctuation
  - ◆ identify the difference between verse and prose
  - ◆ take note of entrances and exits to keep track of who is on stage
  - ◆ pay attention to stage directions
  - ◆ distinguish between speech that takes place between characters and speech that takes place between a character and the audience in an aside or soliloquy.
- Shakespeare's verse is usually unrhymed, with rhyming lines used for emphasis or at the end of key speeches.
- Characters are usually able to switch between speaking in prose or verse depending on who they are talking to and why.
- Prose could be used for speech that is informal, secretive, disrespectful, heart-felt, despairing or fearful – a whole host of subtle emotions.

Comparison

- Possible points of comparison between texts:
  - ◆ key themes
  - ◆ personal response
  - ◆ mood
  - ◆ viewpoint
  - ◆ narrative
  - ◆ setting
  - ◆ type
  - ◆ structure
  - ◆ style
  - ◆ period.

Ideas for starters and plenaries

- Write the title and first line of each poem from the WJEC Literary Heritage Poetry Collection on a small piece of paper and put these into a hat. Students must pick a poem from the hat and then attempt to write the second line. This is a creative exercise rather than a memory test, so students should try to engage with the opening line and create a suitable continuation that is both relevant to the subject matter and in keeping with the poet's style of writing. You could print out a copy of Activity Sheet 1.3.10 to use for this, which includes the titles and first lines of all poems in the collection. Ask students to read out some of their creations and compare these to the actual poems. Discuss the meanings intended by students when writing their versions and the meaning conveyed through the actual versions from the collection.

- Prompt students to draw on their existing knowledge of Shakespeare by working in groups to create a spider diagram containing facts, opinions and contextual references. Divide students into groups of three or four and give each group a sheet of A3 paper. You could prompt students to consider topics such as: why Shakespeare is still studied in schools, best Shakespeare film adaptations, favourite Shakespeare characters, facts about Elizabethan life, biographical facts about Shakespeare and relevant technical terms such as soliloquy, dramatic irony, iambic pentameter, rhyming couplets, tragedy and comedy. Ask students to feed back their ideas to the class. You could also attempt Interactive 1.3.1 as a class, which provides a quiz based on Chapter 1.3 of the Student Book.

- Take each scene in turn from the play that students are studying and pick a group of students to perform the entrances and exits from the scene in front of the class. The stage directions should be read out so that the rest of the class can identify who is who. The 'actors' should perform these snapshots of the action from the play without speaking. They should use body language and distinguishing props or mannerisms to help the audience identify who each person is intended to represent. Activity Sheet 1.3.6 provides further support for this activity and examples from *Twelfth Night*.

- Working in small groups, students should come up with a newspaper-style headline for each scene of the play they are studying. In order to devise a headline that is suitably attention-grabbing, they should consider what the most dramatic events are in the scene. Activity Sheet 1.3.7 provides a template for presenting each headline.

- Ask students to take it in turns to read aloud from 'The Seven Ages of Man' by Shakespeare on page 78 of the Student Book paying close attention to the punctuation. The punctuation has been highlighted in orange in this text so that it stands out. Students should refer to the 'Reading the text' section on page 77 of the Student Book for tips on how to read Shakespeare.

- Give students copies of Activity Sheet 1.3.4, which contains an unpunctuated extract from *Hamlet*. Explain that most punctuation that appears in Shakespeare's texts today has been added by modern editors to help readers understand the text. Students should think carefully about the meaning of each line and insert punctuation where they feel it would be most appropriate. There are clues on the activity sheet to help them. Display Presentation 1.3.10 which contains a punctuated version of the extract and compare this with responses from the student. Discuss similarities and differences and particular features of punctuation in the version displayed.

Lesson ideas

- Discuss the format of the Controlled Assessment using the question and answer material headed 'The Writing Process' on page 89 of the Student Book as a starting point. Presentation 1.3.11 provides additional support for approaching the types of tasks that students are likely to undertake for their assessment. Ask students to then look at the sample tasks provided in Chapter 1.3 of the Student Book. Discuss what each question is asking students to do in each case and what they should aim to cover if they were planning a response to it. Electronic versions of all the example tasks are provided on the OxBox, so they can be easily displayed and annotated on an interactive whiteboard. The sample tasks provided in this chapter of the Teacher's Guide are also available in electronic format in Activity Sheet 1.3.11, which can be displayed or given to students.

- To get students thinking about themes, write one of the eight themes from this unit on the whiteboard, chosen from the following list: love; family and parent-child relationships; youth and age; power and ambition; male-female relationships and the role of women; hypocrisy and prejudice; conflict and grief. Alternatively, you could use Presentation 1.3.9, which includes a screen for each theme. Explain that different writers can approach the same theme from different perspectives – for example, from an optimistic, pessimistic or realistic point of view. For the theme you have displayed, ask students to suggest possible perspectives. Prompt them to provide a mixture of optimistic, pessimistic and rational viewpoints. For example: for 'youth and age', a pessimistic perspective could be: 'young people and old people never understand each other' or an optimistic perspective could be: 'young people can learn a lot from older people'. Consider other themes from the unit. Students could use Activity Sheet 1.3.3 to record their thoughts.

- Look at page 58 of the Student Book, which covers how to read the opening of a poem. Explain why it is important to establish the speaker and situation early on and how a good understanding of the opening lines of a poem can help the reader to develop a deeper insight into the overall text. Students can put this into practise by attempting the activities on pages 59–61 which focus on a number of poems from the WJEC GCSE Poetry Collection. They could use Activity Sheet 1.3.9 to record their thoughts.

- Ask students to look at the 'Themes and words' section on page 81 of the Student Book and the quotations from various Shakespeare plays, which appear on pages 82 to 84. For each quotation, ask students to identify which themes are relevant to it from the following list: love; family and parent-child relationships; youth and age; power and ambition; male-female relationships and the role of women; hypocrisy and prejudice; conflict and grief. You could display Presentation 1.3.8 on the whiteboard for reference, which lists all of these themes.

- Referring again to pages 82 to 84 of the Student Book, select a number of the quotations at random and discuss the themes that students have identified. Ask them to comment on how the theme is dealt with in the quotation. What more can they say about the theme and how it is presented?

- Select an extract from the play that students are studying for this unit and display Presentation 1.3.3. Ask students to work in pairs to answer the questions relating to themes. Students should discuss the questions in their pairs and make notes before feeding back to the class with their ideas. A question sheet is also provided for relationships (Presentation 1.3.4), allowing students to carry out the same activity with a different focus.

- How is the experience of watching a play different to reading a poem or a novel? Ask students to suggest as many ideas as they can think of and write them on the board. Highlight answers such as: the audience actually sees a play and hears the words that the characters speak; the audience experiences the play with other members of the audience; stage directions are acted out; the performance might include sound effects, music or special effects; different performances of the same play may be different because they depend on the decisions of the director; the pace of the performance is determined by the director and the actors rather than the reader.

- Explain that when reading a play, it is important to always think of it as a performance and be aware of how the words on the page might be spoken or acted out on stage. Ask students to look at the section headed 'Entrances and exits' on page 79 of the Student Book. Highlight the point that understanding the significance of a character's speech and actions at a given moment in the play depends upon knowledge of who else is on stage at the same time.

- Pick a theme from the list of themes that relate to this unit (love; family and parent-child relationships; youth and age; power and ambition; male-female relationships and the role of women; hypocrisy and prejudice; conflict and grief). Ask students to work in pairs to select five significant quotations from the play they are studying that reveal something about this theme in the play. You could ask the whole class to work with the same theme, or you could ask different pairs to work with different themes and then feedback to the class. Students could use Activity Sheet 1.3.8 to record their thoughts.

- Discuss the use of verse and prose in Shakespeare with reference to page 79 of the Student Book. Make the point that there are no strict rules associated with verse and prose and that the choice of form is always connected to the specific context of each speech or piece of dialogue. For example, who is speaking to who, what they are talking about, whether the speaker is happy, tense or angry. Students should consider these principles in light of the text they are studying by attempting the activities on page 79. Activity Sheet 1.3.5 provides further support for these activities.

- Look at the activity headed 'Know your characters' on page 80 of the Student Book. Students should draw a larger version of the grid appears on this page or use the template provided on Activity Sheet 1.3.2. In the left-hand column of the grid, students should add names of the characters that appear in the play they are studying, arranged in the order in which they appear. They should then use the rows to the right of this to note down key entrances and exits for each character. The version of the grid in the Student Book sets this out in terms of acts, but this could be broken down into scenes if necessary.

- Referring to the 'Know the plot' section on page 81 of the Student book, ask students to create a bullet-point plot summary of the play that they are studying. For each scene, students should try to capture the most significant points in a few short sentences.

A-A* students should...

- respond critically to texts, identifying subtle links and telling comparisons between them
- present points persuasively and select textual references carefully to back them up, commenting fully on the significant words, phrases and stylistic features
- offer detailed and original interpretations of language patterns, stylistic features and the use of imagery across whole texts
- move confidently between the specific and the general, revealing a clear overview of the texts but also demonstrating the ability to hone in on specific details
- confidently evaluate and comment on character relationships, and characters' attitudes and motives
- structure their responses effectively, with appropriate use of specialist vocabulary and few errors in spelling, punctuation and grammar.

C-B students should...

- respond critically to texts and offer a personal response, referring to aspects of language, grammar and structure to support their views
- select and evaluate textual details confidently and appropriately, demonstrating how writers convey information and meaning through their texts
- compare texts successfully, making cross-references between texts
- convey their ideas clearly and appropriately
- structure their responses appropriately and make good use of specialist vocabulary
- spell most words and punctuate most sentences correctly.

D-E students should...

- respond to the main ideas and themes of the texts
- make simple comparisons and cross-references between texts
- offer a personal response to the text and begin to select relevant and appropriate textual details to support their views
- show some awareness of how writers achieve effects through specific language choices
- structure their responses logically and spell most fundamental words correctly, with some effective use of specialist vocabulary
- punctuate their response appropriately without intrusive errors.

Chapter 1.4a Different Cultures Prose

How to teach GCSE English Literature Unit 1 Section A

AO1

- Respond to texts critically and imaginatively; select and evaluate relevant textual detail to illustrate and support interpretations.

AO2

- Explain how language, structure and form contribute to writers' presentation of ideas, themes and settings.

AO4

- Relate texts to their social, cultural and historical contexts; explain how texts have been influential and significant to self and other readers in different contexts and at different times.

Introduction to the exam

Unit 1 is divided into two sections, which are both assessed by a two-hour exam. For Section A, students will need to study a prose text from a different culture. For Section B, they will write a comparative study on two unseen poems. This chapter focuses on Section A, Different Culture prose. Unit 1 Section B is covered in Chapter 1.2 of this Teacher's Guide.

Section A will require students to answer two questions on their chosen text. The first question (part (a)) will relate to a specific extract from the text that will be printed on the exam paper. The question will ask students to consider a particular aspect of the extract such as how a character is presented or how the writer creates mood and atmosphere. In response to this students will need to produce a close-reading of the extract, ensuring that their answer is closely focused on the text provided.

Students must then select the second question from a choice of two (parts (b) and (c)). These tasks will relate to the text as a whole and will require a response that ranges across the entire novel as appropriate to the question.

The extract question is worth 10 marks and the essay question is worth 20 marks. Students are therefore strongly advised to spend around 20 minutes on part (a) and about 40 minutes on part (b) or part (c). Students are not allowed to take copies of the set texts into the exam with them.

Example exam questions

Students must answer two questions for this section of the exam. The first question (part (a)) will focus on an extract from the set text, which will appear in full on the question paper.

Example questions include:

- With close reference to the extract, show how… presents…
- With close reference to the extract, show how… creates mood and atmosphere here.

Students must then make a choice between part (b) and part (c) and answer one of these questions. Each question will relate to the set text as a whole, so students will be expected to range across the text, as appropriate, in their answer.

Example part (b) questions include:

- How is the character of… presented in the novel?
- Write about the town of… and how it is presented in the novel.
- How are rumours and superstitions important to the novel as a whole?
- How is the character of… important to the novel as a whole?

Example part (c) questions include:

- How is the character of… important to the novel as a whole?
- How does… present the town of… in the novel?
- Show how… makes the reader aware of his/her experiences of racism as he/she grew up, and how he/she learned to cope with these experiences.
- Show how… gradually comes to realise the truth about… in his/her family and in the community.

Key ideas

- Literature from different cultures allows us to see how the wider world works.
- Questions to consider when looking at the opening of a novel:
    - How does the story start?
    - How does it draw the reader in?
    - How much does the writer reveal?
    - Does it give clues as to how the story will develop?
- Readers are likely to react to texts in different ways.
- Suspense can be created through tension, which is an atmosphere of nervousness and unease.
- Mood and atmosphere can be affected by setting and location in the novel.

- The reader is likely to 'sympathize' with a character if:
    - the reader is able to understand the underlying reasons for the character's actions
    - the reader feels that he or she has something in common with the character
    - the reader is able to see events from the character's perspective
    - the reader is able to imagine being in the same situation as the character.
- There are two common types of narrator:
    - third-person narrator – stands outside the story as an observer or commentator
    - first-person narrator – a character within the story.

Ideas for starters and plenaries

- Ask students to read the section headed 'What makes 'different cultures' different?' on page 90 of the Student Book. Why might readers choose to read texts from or about different cultures? What might readers learn from novels set in different places or involving characters from cultures different from their own? Look at the list of bullet points on page 91 of the Student Book. Ask students to identify which of these points are relevant to the text that they are studying for this part of the unit. They could also attempt the activity in the orange box that follows.

- What makes writing funny? Ask students to comment on the kinds of things they find humerous and note some examples on the board. What is the purpose of humour? Why do writers attempt to create it? What can it reveal about a writer, character or the reader? Ask students to suggest aspects from the novel they are studying that they find funny. What is the impact of these episodes on the reader and how do they contribute to the reader's overall understanding of the characters and the situations they face in the novel? Students could then go on to look at the section headed 'Humour' on page 95 of the Student Book and attempt the related activities.

- Explain what is meant by the phrase 'sympathize with'. When reading, hearing or talking about people, what factors are likely to make the reader or listener identify with the person discussed? Draw out points such as recognizing personality traits that they admire, hearing the person's point of view, hearing about a situation that they have been in themselves, or receiving an explanation of the reasons behind a person's actions. Ask students to get into pairs to create a role-play. Explain that they need to create a short dialogue of no more than two minutes in length, which will make one of the characters come across favourably to the audience and the other character come across less favourably. Point out that they will have to use some of the techniques discussed to make the audience sympathize with one of the characters more than the other. Select a number of pairs to present their role-plays to the class. The pair must not introduce the characters or explain who they are; the audience must form their opinions based on the dialogue and actions of the characters alone. Once a dialogue has been performed, the class must then vote on which character they like the most. Did the 'writers' achieve what they intended? Discuss some of the techniques that worked well.

Lesson ideas

- Explain the format of the exam for this unit, pointing out the distinction between the first question, (part (a)), which will be based on an extract from the set text and the second question, (chosen from part (b) or part (c)), which will require students to consider the text as a whole in their response. Explain that for the first question, students will be assessed on their close-reading skills as well as their overall knowledge of the text. Discuss what students understand by the term 'close reading' and how this differs from a more general response. Stress the importance of referring closely to particular language features, the events in the extract, its structure and how it is likely to impact the reader. Students could use Activity Sheet 1.4.1 to practise carrying out a close reading of any of the extracts in Chapter 1.4 of the Student Book in response to the questions provided. Alternatively, they could apply the questions that are relevant, to an extract from the set text they are studying.

- Look at the section headed 'Openings' on page 91 of the Student Book. What does a writer have to do to make a reader curious? Consider the extract on page 92. Read it to the class or ask a student to read it. Discuss the questions in the bullet-point list on page 91 and discuss how they apply to the extract. You could use Activity Sheet 1.4.2 to provide further support for this activity. Ask students to then look at the opening paragraphs of the text that they are studying, either as a class or individually. They could then attempt the second activity on page 92.

- Explain what is meant by giving a personal response in an answer to an exam question, stressing the importance of backing every comment up with evidence from the text and ensuring that what is written is always relevant to the question. Direct students to the section headed 'The reader's response' on page 92 of the Student Book. Ask students to read this section and attempt the activity that follows in response to the extract from *Of Mice and Men*. Students could produce a written response to this extract, or for extra support, they could complete Activity Sheet 1.4.3. This activity sheet includes a number of comments on the passage and students must select the comments that they agree with most strongly, as well as providing evidence for each point they choose. You could then ask students to share some of their ideas with the class and compare responses. Students could then produce a personal response to an extract from a text that they are studying.

- Read the section on suspense that appears on page 93 of the Student Book. Read the extract from *To Kill a Mockingbird* on page 94 as a class and then discuss what makes it tense and dramatic. Highlight how the narrator controls the pace of what happens; firstly demonstrating sharp awareness of movements around her before lapsing into a slow-motion haze, what she describes as a 'dreamlike' experience. Consider how the narrator conveys a sense of inevitability surrounding the jury's verdict. What is the significance of body language in this extract? Why does the narrator focus so closely on how Atticus acts after the verdict? Putting papers into his briefcase and placing his hand on Tom's shoulder? How do these observations create tension in this extract? Ask students to pick out phrases that they think are key to creating atmosphere in this extract and write them on the board.

- Students should look at the section headed 'Feelings' on page 96. Ask students to read the extract on this page and then make five points about how the writer reveals the character's feelings. For extra support, or further practice with linking points to evidence, students could attempt Interactive 1.4.1, which is based on the same extract. This interactive asks students to link points to relevant quotations from the text. Ask students to share some of their points with the class and suggest how they might link these points to the text that they are studying. Students could consolidate this by attempting the second activity on page 96 of the Student Book.

- Direct students to the section headed 'The writer's skills' on page 108 of the Student Book. Explain that lots of factors can contribute to a writer's particular style and that it is possible to comment on specific features of a writer's style in a response to a text. Ask students to answer some of the questions that appear in this paragraph based on the text they are studying for this unit. Take feedback from the group and draw together any common ideas, which help to consolidate an overall impression of the writer's style.

- Explain that a writer's style is heavily related to the narrative style of a text. Discuss features of narrative style using Presentation 1.4.1, which also provides tips and practice questions. Ask students to work in pairs to produce detailed points that they might include in an essay on the narrative of the text that they are studying for this unit. Students should organize their points into a suitable structure for an essay.

A-A* students should...

- present a persuasive and well-structured argument, selecting relevant detail from the text to support their points effectively
- evaluate characters, relationships, attitudes and motives successfully, handling the text with consistency and confidence
- demonstrate the ability to move from the specific to the general when writing about their chosen text
- show appreciation of how writers use language to achieve specific effects and identify stylistic features
- explore the text freely, making an assured evaluation of the ways meaning, ideas and feeling are conveyed through language, structure and form
- show understanding of how texts relate to their social, cultural and historical contexts, linking texts to context where relevant to the question
- use technical vocabulary appropriately and write clearly with few errors in grammar, punctuation and spelling.

C-B students should...

- present a clear and structured argument, making detailed reference to the text
- discuss characters and relationships thoroughly and thoughtfully, handling the text with increasing confidence
- understand and demonstrate how writers use ideas, themes and settings to affect the reader
- demonstrate how writers combine aspects of style and structure to create effects and also identify how writers convey meanings and ideas through language, structure and form
- show understanding of how texts relate to their social, cultural and historical contexts, making valid links that are mostly relevant to the question
- generally use technical vocabulary appropriately and write clearly with only minor errors in spelling or punctuation.

D-E students should...

- present a reasonably clear response with a basic structure, making generalized references to the text
- support the points they make with relevant selections from the text, using paraphrasing and occasional reference to specific details
- make simple comments on particular features of style and structure
- make reference to how texts relate to their social, cultural and historical contexts, with some direct relevance to the question
- write coherently with some non-intrusive errors in grammar, punctuation and spelling and occasional use of appropriate technical vocabulary.

Chapter 1.4b Different Cultures Prose
How to teach GCSE English Unit 3 Section A

AO2

- Read and understand texts, selecting material appropriate to purpose, collating from different sources and making comparisons and cross-references as appropriate.
- Develop and sustain interpretations of writers' ideas and perspectives.
- Explain and evaluate how writers use linguistic, grammatical, structural and presentational features to achieve effects and engage and influence the reader.
- Understand texts in their social, cultural and historical contexts.

Introduction to the Controlled Assessment

Unit 3 is divided into two sections: Section A and Section B. Section A tests reading and Section B tests writing. Both sections are assessed through Controlled Assessment. This chapter focuses on the reading part of the assessment. You can find coverage of the writing section in Chapter 2.1b of this Teacher's Guide.

For Section A, students must submit two assignments. The first assignment will relate to a Shakespeare play and a range of thematically linked heritage poems from the WJEC poetry collection. The requirements of this assignment are covered in more detail in Chapter 1.3a of this guide. This chapter deals with the second assignment for Section A, which requires the study of a different cultures prose text. WJEC will supply tasks for this assignment and they will be released in April of the year before the date of entry for this unit. The tasks will be replaced annually.

Students may carry out their research and planning under limited supervision, which means that teachers may provide them with general advice and they are allowed to work with other students. Students may use the Internet and make use of reference materials during this stage, but they must not write a draft of their response. The final stage of the assessment must be completed under controlled conditions, which means that students must work independently.

They may take a clean copy of the text they have studied into the assessment with them together with one A4 sheet of their own notes prepared in advance. This A4 sheet must not contain a pre-prepared draft or an outline of a response.

Students have up to two hours to complete the final stage of the assessment. Teachers may choose to split this time across separate, shorter sessions but if this is the case, work must be collected in at the end of each session and locked away securely until the start of the next. Following the final session, students may not amend the work they have submitted.

Example reading tasks

Tasks may be presented in the following format:

- How does… present experiences of racism in… community in the novel?
- Show how… makes the reader aware of his/her experiences of prejudice as he/she grew up, and how he/she learned to cope with these experiences.
- How is the character of… important to the novel as a whole?
- Write about the setting of… and how it is presented in the novel.
- How are family relationships important to the novel as a whole?

Key ideas

- Literature from different cultures allows us to see how the wider world works.
- Questions to consider when looking at the opening of a novel:
  - How does the story start?
  - How does it draw the reader in?
  - How much does the writer reveal?
  - Does it give clues as to how the story will develop?
- Readers are likely to react to texts in different ways.
- Suspense can be created through tension, which is an atmosphere of nervousness and unease.
- Mood and atmosphere can be affected by setting and location in the novel.

- The reader is likely to 'sympathize' with a character if:
  - the reader is able to understand the underlying reasons for the character's actions
  - the reader feels that he or she has something in common with the character
  - the reader is able to see events from the character's perspective
  - the reader is able to imagine being in the same situation as the character.
- There are two common types of narrator:
  - third-person narrator – stands outside the story as an observer or commentator
  - first-person narrator – a character within the story.

Ideas for starters and plenaries

- Ask students to read the section headed 'What makes 'different cultures' different?' on page 90 of the Student Book. Why might readers choose to read texts from or about different cultures? What might readers learn from novels set in different places or involving characters from cultures different from their own? Look at the list of bullet points on page 91 of the Student Book. Ask students to identify which of these points are relevant to the text that they are studying. They could also attempt the activity in the orange box that follows.

- What makes writing funny? Ask students to comment on the kinds of things they find humerous and note some examples on the board. What is the purpose of humour? Why do writers attempt to create it? What can it reveal about a writer, character or the reader? Ask students to suggest aspects from the novel they are studying that they find funny. What is the impact of these episodes on the reader and how do they contribute to the reader's overall understanding of the characters and the situations they face in the novel? Students could then go on to look at the section headed 'Humour' on page 95 of the Student Book and attempt the related activities.

- Explain what is meant by the phrase 'sympathize with'. When reading, hearing or talking about people, what factors are likely to make the reader or listener identify with the person discussed? Draw out points such as recognizing personality traits that they admire, hearing the person's point of view, hearing about a situation that they have been in themselves, or receiving an explanation of the reasons behind a person's actions. Ask students to get into pairs to create a role-play. Explain that they need to create a short dialogue of no more than two minutes in length, which will make one of the characters come across favourably to the audience and the other character come across less favourably. Point out that they will have to use some of the techniques discussed to make the audience sympathize with one of the characters more than the other. Select a number of pairs to present their role-plays to the class. The pair must not introduce the characters or explain who they are; the audience must form their opinions based on the dialogue and actions of the characters alone. Once a dialogue has been performed, the class must then vote on which character they like the most. Did the 'writers' achieve what they intended? Discuss on some of the techniques that worked well.

Lesson ideas

- Explain what is meant by giving a personal response in an answer to an exam question, stressing the importance of backing every comment up with evidence from the text and ensuring that what is written is always relevant to the question. Direct students to the section headed 'The reader's response' on page 92 of the Student Book. Ask students to read this section and attempt the activity that follows in response to the extract from *Of Mice and Men*. Students could produce a written response to this extract, or for extra support, they could complete Activity Sheet 1.4.3. This activity sheet includes a number of comments on the passage and students must select the comments that they agree with most strongly, as well as providing evidence for each point they choose. You could then ask students to share some of their ideas with the class and compare responses. Students could then produce a personal response to an extract from a text that they are studying.

- What do students understand by the word 'setting'? Explain that setting is an important factor in all novels as it is likely to have a direct impact on the events of the novel, the plot and the characters, but also the mood and atmosphere, the themes dealt with in the novel and the writer's attitudes to wider issues. Ask students to divide a page into two columns. In the left-hand column they should list as many factors that effect 'setting' as they can think of, such as the geographical location, the weather, the time of day or whether the events take place indoors or outdoors. In the right-hand column ask them to note down details that help to define setting, such as sounds, smells, colours and the feelings and associations experienced by the characters.

- Look at the section headed 'The setting' on page 100 of the Student Book. This section appears in the chapter that deals with Contemporary Prose, but it is also relevant to this chapter. As students to create notes based on these questions with reference to the text that they are studying.

- Ask students to look at the sections headed 'Crisis' and 'The action' on page 103 of the Student Book, the section headed 'The narrator' on page 104 and the section headed 'The ending' on page 111. Then ask students to write a list of brief definitions in their own words for the following terms: plot, cliff-hanger, crisis, pace, twist, suspense, flashback, first-person narrator, third-person narrator, unreliable narrator and open-ended. They should define these terms in relation to narrative structure. Students could alternatively attempt Interactive 1.4.2, which provides a matching exercise where students have to link narrative terms to the correct definitions.

- Direct students to the section headed 'The characters' on page 105 of the Student Book. This section appears in the chapter dealing with Contemporary Prose but it is also relevant to this unit. Divide the class into groups of three or four and give each group a point from the bullet-point list. Ask the group to produce a short presentation applying this question to the text that they are studying for this unit. They could focus on more than one point if necessary. Ask students to build direct references and examples from the text into their presentations.

- Students should look at the section headed 'Feelings' on page 96. Ask students to read the extract on this page and then make five points about how the writer reveals the character's feelings. For extra support, or further practice with linking points to evidence, students could attempt Interactive 1.4.1, which is based on the same extract. This interactive asks students to link points to relevant quotations from the text. Ask students to share some of their points with the class and suggest how they might link these points to the text that they are studying.

- Direct students to the section headed 'The writer's skills' on page 108 of the Student Book. Explain that lots of factors can contribute to a writer's particular style and that it is possible to comment on specific features of a writer's style in a response to a text. Ask students to answer some of the questions that appear in this paragraph based on the text they are studying for this unit. Take feedback from the group and draw together any common ideas, which help to consolidate an overall impression of the writer's style.

- Explain that a writer's style is heavily related to the narrative style of a text. Discuss features of narrative style using Presentation 1.4.1, which also provides tips and practice questions. Ask students to work in pairs to produce detailed points that they might include in an essay on the narrative of the text that they are studying for this unit. Students should to organize their points into a suitable structure for an essay.

A-A* students should...

- be able to select material appropriate to purpose and make valid comments and inferences based on the texts they read
- be able to respond to the detail as well as an overview of the text
- develop and sustain an interpretation of the writer's ideas and perspectives, selecting relevant points and explaining them with a clear depth of understanding
- successfully analyse the linguistic, grammatical, structural and presentational techniques used by each writer to create particular effects
- show a clear understanding of the relevant social, cultural and historical contexts and identify the significance of these contexts when forming an interpretation of the text
- be able to relate the texts to their own and other's experience
- show an awareness of relevant literary traditions and how texts have been and continue to be influential at different times.

C-B students should...

- be able to select material appropriate to purpose and make valid comments and inferences based on the texts they read
- develop an interpretation of the writer's ideas and perspectives, selecting relevant points and explaining most of them with some depth of understanding
- analyse the linguistic, grammatical, structural and presentational techniques used by the writer and begin to address the question of 'how' each writer achieves particular effects
- be able to relate texts to the relevant social, cultural and historical contexts and begin to appreciate how texts have been and continue to be influential
- begin to relate the texts to their own and others' experiences.

D-E students should...

- be able to select material appropriate to purpose and make simple comments on the surface features of the text
- show some awareness of the more obvious implicit meanings of the text
- make appropriate points about the writer's ideas and perspectives with some comment
- offer some comment on the linguistic, grammatical, structural and presentational techniques used by the writer with reference to the text
- show some basic awareness of related social, cultural and historical contexts and how these contexts are relevant to understanding the text.

Chapter 1.5a Prose and Drama
How to teach GCSE English Literature Unit 2a

AO1

- Respond to texts critically and imaginatively; select and evaluate relevant textual detail to illustrate and support interpretations.

AO2

- Explain how language, structure and form contribute to writers' presentation of ideas, themes and settings.

AO4

- Relate texts to their social, cultural and historical contexts; explain how texts have been influential and significant to self and other readers in different contexts and at different times.

Introduction to the exam

Unit 2 is assessed by a two-hour exam and is divided into two sections. Students can either write on literary heritage drama and contemporary prose (Unit 2a) or contemporary drama and literary heritage prose (Unit 2b). Both sections of the exam will ask students to answer two questions on each of the two texts that they have studied for this unit. In each case, the first question will ask students to produce a close reading in relation to an extract from the text. The extract will be printed on the exam question paper and the question will be worth 10 marks. The second question, chosen from two further options, will ask students to relate their answer to the text as a whole. This question will be worth 20 marks.

Students are advised to divide their time equally between the texts they have studied; so they should spend one hour answering both questions on the first set text and one hour answering both questions on the second set text. They will not be asked to compare the texts in any of the questions on this paper.

Students are not allowed to take copies of their set texts into the exam with them. This chapter of the Teacher's Guide deals with Unit 2a. Unit 2b is covered in more detail in Chapter 1.5b.

Example exam questions

Students will be required to answer two questions on each set text that they have studied for this unit. For each text, the first task (part (i)) will ask them to answer a question based on an extract from the set text, which will be printed on the exam paper. Students will then have a choice of two questions for the second task (parts (ii) and (iii)). Both options will ask students to write about the set text in full. The questions that follow represent examples of what might appear in each part of the exam:

Literary heritage drama text

Part (i) – *Close-reading question*

- Look closely at how… and… speak and behave here. What does it reveal about their relationship?

- Look closely at how… and… speak and behave here. What impressions would an audience receive of their characters?

- Look closely at how… speaks and behaves here. How could it affect an audience's feelings towards him/her?

- With close reference to the extract, show how it reveals the relationship between… and… at this point in the play.
- Look closely at how… and… speak and behave here. How does it create mood and atmosphere for an audience?

Part (ii) – *General question*

- Why does… behave…?
- Show how… presents the development of the relationship between… and…
- The play is set in…, and was written in the… Why do you think it is still popular today, in the 21st century? Remember to support your answer with reference to the text.
- Why do you think… called his/her play…? To what extent do you find it an appropriate title for the play?

Part (iii) – *General question*

- How does… present the character… to an audience throughout the play?
- How is/are… important to the play as a whole?

Contemporary prose text

Part (i) – *Close-reading question*

- With close reference to the extract, show how… suggests… feelings here.
- With close reference to the extract, show how… creates mood and atmosphere here.

Part (ii) – *General question*

- Show how… relationship with… is presented throughout the novel.
- To what extent is… an effective title for this novel, in your opinion?
- Of the central characters… with whom do you have the most sympathy and why? Show how… presentation of your chosen character creates sympathy for him or her.
- Write about… and the way he/she is presented in the novel.
- What do you think of… and the way he/she is presented in the novel?

Part (iii) – *General question*

- What do you think of… and the way he/she is presented in the novel?
- How effective a title is… in your opinion?

Key ideas

Contemporary prose

- Novels written between in the late 20th and early 21st century are regarded as 'contemporary'.
- Contemporary novels may focus on events from the past and may therefore deal with earlier periods as a subject matter.
- Questions to ask when considering setting:
    - Where does the story take place?
    - How much information is the reader given about the setting?
    - What is the importance of the setting?
    - Does the setting help to create a particular mood or atmosphere?

- The reader can learn a lot about characters through:
    - dialogue – what the characters say and how they say it
    - tone – the way the narrator describes the characters – for example, with sympathy, fondness or cold detachment
    - actions – what the characters do
    - other characters – what is said about them and how others behave towards them
    - dilemma – when characters have to make difficult decisions
    - crisis – when events in the plot take a dramatic turn
    - development – how characters change as the story progresses.

Key ideas (continued...)

- Questions to think about when considering the events of the novel:
  - What are the key events?
  - Are there twists and cliff-hangers?
  - Does the writer deliberately hold back information about events to create mystery?
  - Is the plot fast or slow-paced?
  - What period of time is covered by the story?
- Things to think about when forming a personal response:
  - Did anything strike you or surprise you about the text?
  - What have you learned from it?
  - Has it changed your opinions in any way?
  - What is your attitude to the writer after reading the story?
- There are two common types of narrator:
  - third-person narrator – stands outside the story as an observer or commentator
  - first-person narrator – a character within the story.

Literary heritage drama

- Literary heritage drama covers influential drama written before the late 20th century.
- Questions to ask when thinking about the action of drama texts:
  - What are the key events of the play?
  - Are there any twists or cliff-hangers?
  - Does the writer deliberately hold back information from the audience to create mystery?
  - Is the plot fast-moving or slow-paced?
  - What period of time is covered by the action?

- The audience can learn a lot about characters through:
  - dialogue – what the characters say and how they say it
  - stage directions – what the characters do
  - other characters – what is said about them and how others behave towards them
  - dilemma – when characters have to make difficult decisions
  - crisis – when events in the plot take a dramatic turn
  - development – how characters change as the play progresses.
- Points to think about when considering setting:
  - Where does the action take place?
  - Does the writer describe the setting in detail?
  - Is the stage expected to be precisely arranged?
  - Does the action of the play move between settings?
  - What is the significance of the setting(s)?
  - Does the setting influence the mood or atmosphere?
  - What theatrical tricks or surprises are evident?
- Points to think about when considering the ending:
  - How does the play end?
  - Is it a satisfying ending?
  - Does the play end as expected?
  - Does the writer leave any questions unanswered?
  - Has the mood and atmosphere changed over the course of the play?
- A soliloquy is a speech spoken by a character alone on stage or at least out of earshot of other characters.

Ideas for starters and plenaries

- In pairs, students should produce an A3-sized poster summarizing key points about the setting of the novel they are studying. They could refer to the questions that appear in the section headed 'The setting' on page 100 of the Student Book for ideas about what to include on the poster. If possible, they could also select and include images, which help them to visualize the setting and themes associated with it in the novel. They could carry out a similar activity for the literary heritage play that they are studying with reference to the section headed 'The setting' on page 117, which deals specifically with drama.
- Ask students to work in groups of three to create an eight-part flow chart detailing the events that make up the main 'action' in the play or novel that they are studying. A template for a suitable chart is available with Activity Sheet 1.5.3, which can be adapted to best suit the text that students are studying. Students

should first discuss what they feel are the eight most significant events in the text giving reasons for their thoughts. They should then arrange these events into the correct order in which they occur and add a brief summary of each one to the flow chart. Following this, students should then add notes or symbols to the lines that connect the boxes to indicate some or all of the following: 1) any cliffhangers that occur between the events, 2) twists in the plot, 3) where the narrative moves slowly, 4) where the narrative seems to speed up, 5) where there is a build-up of suspense. Ask each group to feed their ideas back to the class.

- What can be said about the narrator of the contemporary prose text that students are studying? Ask students to create a profile of the narrator (or narrators) based on the questions raised in the sections headed 'The narrator' and 'Mystery' on page 104 of the Student Book. They could set this up in a question and answer format, or use sub-headings based on the points covered in these sections. They could also include any facts about the narrator's identity, if this information is given in the text, such as the narrator's name, age, occupation, and links with other characters in the novel. They could even include an avatar that best represents their view of the narrator. A template for this activity is provided with Activity Sheet 1.5.7.

Lesson ideas

- Explain the format of the exam for this unit, pointing out the distinction between the first question on each set text (part (i)), which will be based on an extract and the second question (chosen from part (ii) or part (iii)), which will require students to consider each text as a whole in their response. Explain that for the first question, students will be assessed on their close-reading skills as well as their overall knowledge of each text. Discuss what students understand by the term 'close reading' and how this differs from a more general response. Stress the importance of referring closely to particular language features, the events in the extract, its structure and how it is likely to impact the reader. Students could use Activity Sheet 1.5.1 to practise carrying out a close reading of any of the extracts in Chapters 1.5.1 and 1.5.3 of the Student Book in response to the questions provided. Alternatively, they could apply the questions that are relevant, to an extract from the set text they are studying.

- Why do writers choose to write about childhood? Discuss this topic with the class and encourage students to put forward as many ideas as possible. Perhaps highlight points such as building a strong sense of character development, providing a background for the main events in the novel, establishing a connection between the reader and the character, reflecting on events from a perspective different from that of the reader, revealing the challenges and hardships faced by those who do not always have a voice in society. Next look at the section headed 'Childhood' on page 101 of the Student Book. Ask students to carry out a close reading of the extract from *Paddy Clarke Ha Ha Ha*, focusing on how the writer attempts to convey the experience of childhood. Activity Sheet 1.5.2 provides further support for this activity by providing points that students need to link to relevant quotations from the text. This activity sheet is also available in electronic form in Interactive 1.5.1. Having worked with the *Paddy Clarke* extract, students could then go on to attempt the second activity on page 101 in response to the contemporary prose text that they are studying.

- Ask students to read the section headed 'The characters' on page 116 of the Student Book. This list of questions summarizes the kinds of issues that students may be expected to think about when writing about character in their exam. Divide the class into small groups and give each group one question from this list. You could give each group more than one question if necessary. Ask students to produce a short presentation based on the question, building in references and examples from the text to support their points. Each group should then present their presentation to the class. Alternatively, each group could work together to produce a list of three points in response to their given question/s. They could submit these to the teacher, who could then select the best points and present these to the class, adding extra detail where necessary or asking for elaboration from the groups on certain issues.

- Direct students to the sections of main text headed 'The narrator', 'Mystery', 'Dilemma' and 'Crisis' on pages 102 to 104 of the Student Book. Alternatively, you could display Presentation 1.5.2, which includes a summary of this content. Ask students to then consider and comment on the role of the narrator in the extracts of contemporary prose that appear on pages 102, 103 and 104. For further support, you could provide students with Activity Sheet 1.5.8, which provides students with three example responses. When working with the activity sheets, students must decide which response relates to which extract and then develop each response with their own ideas and evidence from the extracts. Provide students with an extract from the novel that they are studying and ask them to produce a close-reading focusing on the role of the narrator in this passage.

- Explain that scenes of 'revelation', 'hostility', and 'disagreement' often reveal a lot about individual characters. Ask students to read the sections of main text that appear under these headings in Chapter 1.5.3 of the Student Book. They should then vote for the topic they want to look at in more detail. Look at the extract that corresponds to the chosen topic and select students to read the various parts. As a class, discuss the question that appears in the related activity box. Encourage students to share as many ideas as possible and prompt them to pick out examples from the extract to support their points. You could repeat this activity for the next topic, working as a class and then ask students to consider the final topic on their own. Further support for each activity is provided in Activity Sheet 1.5.4, Activity Sheet 1.5.5 and Activity Sheet 1.5.6. Each activity sheet provides a series of points relating to the extracts from the Student Book. Students must first decide whether they agree or disagree with each of the points and then link their chosen points to appropriate evidence from the text.

- Following the activity above, students could think about how the themes of 'revelation', 'hostility' and 'disagreement' apply to the play that they are studying. Ask them to list as many examples of 'revelation' that they can think of that occur in their set play, and ask them to do the same for 'hostility' and 'disagreement'. They could consolidate their knowledge by attempting the activities on pages 116, 117 and 118, which refer them directly to the play that they are studying.

- Discuss what is meant by 'dramatic technique' and how to approach this topic when it appears in an exam question. Presentation 1.5.1 includes key points to consider. Ask students to look at the following sections of Chapter 1.5.3 in the Student Book: 'Revelation', 'Hostility', 'The setting' and 'Disagreement'. For each section ask them to read the text and list specific examples from the play they are studying that help to illustrate these points and techniques. They could carry out a similar exercise using the following sections of Chapter 1.5.4 in the Student Book: 'The writer's skills', 'Decisions' and 'The reader/audience'.

- Having discussed the format of questions focusing on 'dramatic technique', ask students to work in pairs to produce detailed points that they might use when answering this type of question on the text they are studying. Presentation 1.5.1 also includes sample questions.

A-A* students should...

- present a persuasive and well-structured argument, selecting relevant details from the text to support their points effectively
- evaluate characters, relationships, attitudes and motives successfully, handling the text with consistency and confidence
- demonstrate the ability to move from the specific to the general when writing about their chosen text
- show appreciation of how writers use language to achieve specific effects and identify stylistic features
- explore the text freely, making an assured evaluation of the ways meaning, ideas and feeling are conveyed through language, structure and form
- show understanding of how texts relate to their social, cultural and historical contexts, linking texts to context where relevant to the question
- use technical vocabulary appropriately and write clearly with few errors in grammar, punctuation and spelling.

C-B students should...

- present a clear and structured argument, making detailed reference to the text
- discuss characters and relationships thoroughly and thoughtfully, handling the text with increasing confidence
- understand and demonstrate how writers use ideas, themes and settings to affect the reader
- demonstrate how writers combine aspects of style and structure to create effects and identify how writers convey meanings and ideas through language, structure and form
- show understanding of how texts relate to their social, cultural and historical contexts, making valid links that are mostly relevant to the question
- generally use technical vocabulary appropriately and write clearly with only minor errors in spelling or punctuation.

D-E students should...

- present a reasonably clear response with a basic structure, making generalized references to the text
- support the points they make with relevant selections from the text, using paraphrasing and occasional reference to specific details
- make simple comments on particular features of style and structure
- make reference to how texts relate to their social, cultural and historical contexts, with some direct relevance to the question
- write coherently with some non-intrusive errors in grammar, punctuation and spelling and occasional use of appropriate technical vocabulary.

Chapter 1.5b Prose and Drama
How to teach GCSE English Literature Unit 2b

AO1

- Respond to texts critically and imaginatively; select and evaluate relevant textual detail to illustrate and support interpretations.

AO2

- Explain how language, structure and form contribute to writers' presentation of ideas, themes and settings.

AO4

- Relate texts to their social, cultural and historical contexts; explain how texts have been influential and significant to self and other readers in different contexts and at different times.

Introduction to the exam

Unit 2 is assessed by a two-hour exam and is divided into two sections. Students can either write on literary heritage drama and contemporary prose (Unit 2a) or contemporary drama and literary heritage prose (Unit 2b). Both sections of the exam will ask students to answer two questions on each of the two texts that they have studied for this unit. In each case, the first question will ask students to produce a close reading of an extract from the text. The extract will be printed on the exam question paper and the question will be worth 10 marks. The second question, chosen from two options, will ask students to relate their answer to the text as a whole. This question will be worth 20 marks.

Students are advised to divide their time equally between the texts they have studied; so they should spend one hour answering both questions on the first set text and one hour answering both questions on the second set text. They will not be asked to compare the texts in any of the questions on this paper.

Students are not allowed to take copies of their set texts into the exam with them. This chapter of the Teacher's Guide deals with Unit 2b. Unit 2a is covered in more detail in Chapter 1.5a.

Example exam questions

Students will be required to answer two questions on each set text that they have studied for this unit. For each text, the first task (part (i)) will ask them to answer a question based on an extract from the set text, which will be printed on the exam paper. Students will then have a choice of two questions to choose from for the second task, (parts (ii) and (iii)). Both options will ask students to write about the set text in full. The questions that follow represent examples of what might appear in each part of the exam:

Contemporary drama text

Part (i) – *Close-reading question*

- Look closely at how… speaks and behaves here. What does it reveal about his/her character?
- Look closely at how the characters speak and behave here. How does it create mood and atmosphere for an audience?
- With close reference to the extract, show how… creates mood and atmosphere for an audience here.
- Look closely at how… speaks and behaves here. What does it reveal about his/her feelings?

Part (ii) – *General question*

- How does… present the character of… to an audience throughout the play?
- To what extent do you feel sympathy for…?
- What do you think of… and the way he/she is presented in the play?

Part (iii) – *General question*

- How does… show changes in women's lives during the twentieth century in the play?
- Write about the way the theme of… is presented in the play.
- There are many emotions in this play: love; hatred; jealousy; anger. Write about **one** of these emotions and how it is presented.

Literary heritage prose text

Part (i) – *Close-reading question*

- With close reference to the extract, show how… creates mood and atmosphere here.
- Look closely at how… presents the character of… here. How does it influence the reader's attitude towards her/him?

Part (ii) – *General question*

- How is the relationship between… and… presented in the novel?
- Show how… presents the hardships of… in the novel.
- What do you think of… and the way he/she is presented in the novel?
- How does… present… relationships with…?

Part (iii) – *General question*

- How is… important to the novel as a whole?
- How does… present the theme of… in the novel?
- How does… present… changing character in the novel?
- A review of… said… To what extent do you agree? Remember to support your answer with detailed reference to the text.

Key ideas

Literary heritage prose

- Literary Heritage prose includes influential works of fiction and non-fiction written before the late 20th century.
- Questions to ask when considering setting:
  - Where and when does the story take place?
  - How much detail does the writer reveal about the setting?
  - Does the setting influence the mood or atmosphere of the text?
  - What does the setting reveal about the time in which the text was written?
- The reader can learn a lot about characters through:
  - dialogue – what the characters say and how they say it
  - tone – the way the narrator describes the characters – for example, with sympathy, fondness or cold detachment
  - actions – what the characters do
  - other characters – what is said about them and how others behave towards them
  - dilemma – when characters have to make difficult decisions
  - crisis – when events in the plot take a dramatic turn.
- The writer's style may be characterized by specific choices regarding:
  - sentence types
  - choice of vocabulary
  - the balance between description and dialogue
  - the tone and voice of the narrator
  - patterns of imagery
  - level of detail
  - use of humour.

Key ideas (continued...)

- Questions to ask when considering the ending of the text:
  - How does the text end?
  - Is it a satisfying ending?
  - Does the text end as expected?
  - Does the writer leave any questions unanswered?
  - Has the mood and atmosphere changed during the story?
- Questions to think about when considering the themes of the text:
  - What themes is the writer interested in?
  - Does the writer move from the specifics of the characters and events to reflect on life in general?
  - Are the writer's ideas still relevant to life today?
  - Is the writer optimistic (hopeful) or pessimistic (not hopeful) about the ideas he or she expresses in the text?

Drama – Contemporary

- Contemporary drama could include plays written in the second half of the 20th century as well as those written in the 21st century.
- It deals with modern issues and is often controversial.
- Dramatic irony occurs when the audience is aware of something but the characters in the play are not.
- Points to consider when looking at the structure of the play:
  - How many acts and scenes are there in the play?
  - Is the play heavy or light on stage directions?

- Is there a narrator?
- Do characters speak at length about their thoughts through soliloquies?
- Are there any sub-plots?
- Are there any moments of dramatic irony in the play?
- Conflict is a common theme in contemporary drama and can govern the progress of the plot.
- The conflict of contemporary drama is often the result of:
  - differences between characters from different generations
  - a dispute over who holds power and authority.
- Questions to think about when considering the themes of the text:
  - What themes is the writer interested in?
  - Does the writer move from the specifics of the characters and events to reflect on life in general?
  - Are the writer's ideas still relevant to life today?
  - Is the writer optimistic (hopeful) or pessimistic (not hopeful) about the ideas he or she expresses through the play?
- Things to think about when forming a personal response:
  - Did anything strike you or surprise you about the play?
  - What have you learned from it?
  - Has it changed your opinions in any way?
  - What is your attitude to the writer after studying the play?

Ideas for starters and plenaries

- In pairs, students should produce an A3-sized poster summarizing key points about the setting of the novel they are studying. They could refer to the section headed 'The setting' on page 108 of the Student Book for ideas about what to include on the poster. If possible, they could also select and include images, which help them to visualize the setting and themes associated with it in the novel. They could carry out a similar activity for the contemporary play that they are studying with reference to the section headed 'The setting' on page 117, which deals specifically with drama.

- Ask students to work in groups of three to create an eight-part flow chart detailing the events that make up the main 'action' in the play or novel that they are studying. A template for a suitable chart is available with Activity Sheet 1.5.3, which can be adapted to best suit the text that students are studying. Students should first discuss what they feel are the eight most significant events in the text giving reasons for their thoughts. They should then arrange these events into the correct order in which they occur and add a brief summary of each one to the flow chart. Following this, students should then add notes or symbols to the lines that connect the boxes to indicate some or all of the following: 1) any cliffhangers that occur between the events, 2) twists in the plot, 3) where the narrative moves slowly, 4) where the narrative seems to speed up, 5) where there is a build-up of suspense. Ask each group to feed their ideas back to the class.

● What can be said about the narrator of the literary heritage prose text that students are studying? Ask students to create a profile of the narrator (or narrators) based on the questions raised in the sections headed 'The narrator' on page 104 of the Student Book as well as the sections headed 'Confused emotions' and 'The writer's ideas' on page 111 of the Student Book. Students could set the profile up in a question and answer format, or use sub-headings based on the points covered in these sections. They could also include any facts about the narrator's identity, if this information is given in the text, such as the narrator's name, age, occupation, and links with other characters in the novel. They could even include an avatar that best represents their view of the narrator. A template for this activity is provided with Activity Sheet 1.5.7.

Lesson ideas

● Explain the format of the exam for this unit, pointing out the distinction between the first question on each set text (part (i)), which will be based on an extract and the second question (chosen from part (ii) or part (iii)), which will require students to consider each text as a whole in their response. Explain that for the first question, students will be assessed on their close-reading skills as well as their overall knowledge of each text. Discuss what students understand by the term 'close reading' and how this differs from a more general response. Stress the importance of referring closely to particular language features, the events in the extract, its structure and how it is likely to impact the reader. Students could use Activity Sheet 1.5.1 to practise carrying out a close reading of any of the extracts in Chapters 1.5.2 and 1.5.4 of the Student Book in response to the questions provided. Alternatively, they could apply the questions that are relevant, to an extract from the set text they are studying.

● What do students understand by the term 'Literary Heritage Prose'? Discuss their ideas with reference to the introductory section of main text that appears on page 106 of the Student Book. Then consider the section headed 'The time in which the text was written/set' on page 109, which deals with some of the implications of studying a literary heritage text. What can be said about the text that students are studying in relation to these points? Ask student to suggest examples selected from the events, characters and themes of the novel that help to elucidate these points.

● Ask students to read the section headed 'The writer's skills' on page 108. Students should then work in groups of three to come up with two points in answer to each question that features under this heading, in relation to the text that they are studying. Remind students that they should support these points by picking one or two quotations from the text or by referring to specific parts of the text. Go through the questions as a class, asking the groups to contribute their ideas. You could add some of these to the whiteboard.

● Look at the introductory section headed 'What is 'contemporary' drama?' on page 120 of the Student Book and then direct students to the section headed 'Lives' a little further down the page. Emphasize that contemporary drama is often concerned with the everyday lives of ordinary people, linking actions and events to wider themes and reflections upon society. Select students to read the extract from *My Mother Said I Never Should* on pages 120 to 121 of the Student Book, allocating parts as necessary. Discuss, as a class, what themes are raised in this extract and how the dramatist attempts to confront them through the actions and dialogue of the characters. Further support for this activity is provided with Activity Sheet 1.5.9, which include a series of prompts for discussion.

- Explain that scenes involving a battle for control, complex discussions and crucial decisions often reveal a lot about important themes in the play. Ask students to read the sections of main text entitled 'Control', 'Discussion' and 'Decisions' in Chapter 1.5.4 of the Student Book. They should then vote for the topic they want to look at in more detail. Look at the extract that corresponds to the chosen topic and select students to read the various parts. As a class, discuss the question that appears in the related activity box. Encourage students to share as many ideas as possible and prompt them to pick out examples from the extract to support their points. You could repeat this activity for the next topic, working as a class and then ask students to consider the final topic on their own. Further support for each activity is provided in Activity Sheet 1.5.10, Activity Sheet 1.5.11 and Activity Sheet 1.5.12. Each activity sheet provides a series of points relating to the extracts from the Student Book. Students must first decide whether they agree or disagree with each point and then decide what each one might reveal about the wider themes of the play as a whole.

- Explain what is meant by giving a personal response in an answer to an exam question, stressing the importance of backing every comment up with evidence from the text and ensuring that what is written is always relevant to the question. Direct students to the section headed 'The reader/audience' on page 126 of the Student Book. Ask students to answer the questions that appear in this section in relation to the text they have studied for this unit and then discuss, as a class, how they might build some of these thoughts and ideas into a response to an exam question.

- Discuss what is meant by 'dramatic technique' and how to approach this topic when it appears in an exam question. Presentation 1.5.1 includes key points to consider. Ask students to look at the following sections of Chapter 1.5.3 in the Student Book: 'Revelation', 'Hostility', 'The setting' and 'Disagreement'. For each section ask them to read the text and list specific examples from the play they are studying that help to illustrate these points and techniques. They could carry out a similar exercise using the following sections of Chapter 1.5.4 in the Student Book: 'The writer's skills', 'Decisions' and 'The reader/audience'.

- Having discussed the format of questions focusing on 'dramatic technique', ask students to work in pairs to produce detailed points that they might use when answering this type of question on the text they are studying. Presentation 1.5.1 also includes sample questions.

A-A* students should...

- present a persuasive and well-structured argument, selecting relevant detail from the text to support their points effectively
- evaluate characters, relationships, attitudes and motives successfully, handling the text with consistency and confidence
- demonstrate the ability to move from the specific to the general when writing about their chosen text
- show appreciation of how writers use language to achieve specific effects and identify stylistic features
- explore the text freely, making an assured evaluation of the ways meaning, ideas and feeling are conveyed through language, structure and form
- show understanding of how texts relate to their social, cultural and historical contexts, linking texts to context where appropriate to the question
- use technical vocabulary appropriately and write clearly with few errors in grammar, punctuation and spelling.

C-B students should...

- present a clear and structured argument, making detailed reference to the text
- discuss characters and relationships thoroughly and thoughtfully, handling the text with increasing confidence
- understand and demonstrate how writers use ideas, themes and settings to affect the reader
- demonstrate how writers combine aspects of style and structure to create effects and identify how writers convey meanings and ideas through language, structure and form
- show understanding of how texts relate to their social, cultural and historical contexts, making valid links that are mostly relevant to the question
- generally use technical vocabulary appropriately and write clearly with only minor errors in spelling or punctuation.

D-E students should...

- present a reasonably clear response with a basic structure, making generalized references to the text
- support the points they make with relevant selections from the text, using paraphrasing and occasional reference to specific details
- make simple comments on particular features of style and structure
- make reference to how texts relate to their social, cultural and historical contexts, with some direct relevance to the question
- write coherently with some non-intrusive errors in grammar, punctuation and spelling and occasional use of appropriate technical vocabulary.

Chapter 2.1a Creative Writing
How to teach GCSE English Language Unit 3 Section B

AO4

- Write to communicate clearly, effectively and imaginatively, using and adapting forms and selecting vocabulary appropriate to task and purpose in ways which engage the reader.
- Organize information and ideas into structured and sequenced sentences, paragraphs and whole texts, using a variety of linguistic and structural features to support cohesion and overall coherence.
- Use a range of sentence structures for clarity, purpose and effect, with accurate punctuation and spelling.

Introduction to the Controlled Assessment

Unit 3 is assessed through Controlled Assessment, which replaces traditional GCSE coursework. Unlike the examined units, it is not split into Foundation and Higher tier papers.

For Section B, students are expected to submit two tasks; a piece of descriptive writing and a piece of narrative/expressive writing. WJEC will supply these tasks and they will be replaced every year. Responses must be in written form.

During the research and planning stage of the assessment, students may work under informal supervision and may refer to resources and stimulus materials relevant to their chosen tasks. The final pieces of writing must then be completed under controlled conditions in no more than two hours.

The time available for the final writing session may be split across shorter sessions. Students must hand their work in at the end of each session and this should be locked away until the next session begins.

Example writing tasks

Students will be asked to complete one descriptive task and one narrative/expressive task.

Descriptive tasks may include:

- Describe the scene at…
- Write a description of…
- Describe a place that…
- Describe a person who…
- Describe what you see and hear as…

Narrative/expressive tasks may include:

- Write about a time when…
- Continue the following…
- Write about an incident which…
- Write a story which is set in…
- An evocative title for a piece of writing such as: *The Rescue, The Visitor, Jealousy* or *The Traitor.*

- Descriptive writing focuses on a place or person (key word = focus).
- Narrative writing is an account of connective events (key word = control).
- Features of good descriptive writing:
  - engaging content
  - effective organization
  - detail and thoughtful vocabulary.
- Features of good narrative writing:
  - well-judged plot and characters
  - good beginning and appropriate ending

- purposeful and well-paced
- paragraphs varied in length with appropriate connectives
- the reader's interest is held..

- Features of accurate writing:
  - sentences are varied and controlled
  - punctuation is used to clarify meaning and create effects
  - spelling of both simple and complex vocabulary is correct
  - grammar is used confidently and purposefully.

Ideas for starters and plenaries

- Ask students to suggest as many ideas as they can about what makes a good opening and write them on the board. Once a number of ideas has been collected, ask students to rate each idea from 1 to 3 according to the impact they feel it will have on an opening. They should vote for the rating they feel is most appropriate. '1' could represent 'vital', '2' could represent 'very important' and '3' could represent 'a nice touch'.

- Display one or more stimulus images included in Presentation 2.1.2 and ask students to describe the scene in each image. Ask the class to suggest words to describe the action and mood of the scene.

- Watch clips of the last few minutes of two popular films. If necessary, give a brief summary of what each film is about, what has happened in the immediate lead-up to the final scenes and who the key characters are. Ask students to comment on how they feel about each ending. What do they think works well about the ending? What is disappointing about it? What techniques does the scriptwriter/director use to signal that this is the conclusion of the narrative? Does the ending tie everything up neatly or leave some questions unanswered? Explain that when writing a conclusion to their own narratives, students will have to make similar choices.

- Read students the extracts on page 136 of the Student Book and ask them to come up with paragraphs of bad 'genre' writing of their own.

- Work as a class to develop three descriptions of a scene. Display a very basic description of a scene on the board or use Presentation 2.1.6. Ask students to contribute details to the description to make the scene more interesting and more lifelike. Add suggestions to the board. Ask students to write an improved version of the descriptive scene, building in some of these ideas.

Lesson ideas

- Turn to the section headed 'What makes a good piece of descriptive writing?' on page 133 of the Student Book and ask students to consider the first point. What techniques can writers use to make their descriptive writing 'engaging' and 'interesting' to the reader? Pull out points such as managing the level of detail, using humour or suspense, using vivid imagery and well-chosen vocabulary and engaging the senses. Discuss the tasks that appear in the bullet-point list on page 133. How would students go about writing an engaging and interesting response to each task in light of what has been discussed? Ask students to put some of these ideas into practice by writing an opening sentence for each task.

- Turn to page 134 of the Student Book and ask students to consider the example paragraph of descriptive writing at the top of the page. How has the writer chosen to structure this piece of writing and what is effective about it? How else could the writer have approached this paragraph? Try re-ordering the text. What effects do these changes have on focus and tone? Ask students to write an opening paragraph for one of the tasks on the same page. Students should then swap their work with a partner and feed back. How well has each writer structured the piece of writing? What works well and what could be improved?

- Explain the importance of striking a balance in terms of level of detail in descriptive writing. What is likely to be the negative effect of adding too much detail to a piece of description? What about not including enough detail? Discuss methods by which writers can build detail into their writing such as selecting the best vocabulary, using imagery and engaging the senses. Highlight the point that adding more detail does not necessarily mean writing lots of extra text. Ask students to attempt the activity on page 135 of the Student Book to improve the level of detail used in each sentence. Build on this activity by discussing how writers can control the level of detail to draw attention to things that he or she would like the reader to focus on.

- Display selected examples of descriptive writing from the Student Book on the whiteboard and read them through with the class. All of these are included in electronic form on the OxBox. Alternatively, you could use the supplimentary extracts provided in Presentation 2.1.1. Remind them of the features of good descriptive writing. Taking each extract in turn, ask students to work in pairs to list the positive qualities of each extract and then ask each pair to feed back to the class. They could use the grid provided in Activity Sheet 2.1.1 to record their ideas.

- Provide students with two examples of descriptive writing, produced in response to the same task. For example, you could select two descriptions of a dentist's waiting room from page 135 of the Student Book. These extracts can be displayed on the whiteboard using Presentation 2.2.4. Alternatively, you could hand out copies of Activity Sheet 2.1.6, which includes two responses to the task: 'Describe the scene in a large shopping centre on Christmas Eve.' Ask students to work in pairs to compare and contrast the responses. Students could use the grids provided on Activity Sheet 2.1.7 to record their thoughts.

- After students have evaluated both pieces of writing, ask them to produce a list of five top tips for answering this question effectively. Ask pairs to feed back to the class with their thoughts about both pieces of writing and their tips for success.

- Display Presentation 2.2.5, which includes comments from the examiner on the three descriptions of a dentist's waiting room that feature on page 135 of the Student Book. Alternatively, display Presentation 2.2.3, which includes an examiner's comment on the extracts from Activity Sheet 2.1.6. Discuss this feedback with the class. Is there anything students would like to add to their list of tips having considered these remarks?

- Go through the features of good narrative writing using the responses in the Student Book as exemplars. Students can build confidence in incorporating these features into their own writing through attempting the activities on pages 137–138. Use Activity Sheet 2.1.5 to allow students to put their skills to the test. This activity sheet includes a badly-structured narrative in need of a makeover.

- Ask students to work in groups of five or six to put together a narrative as a group. Give each group a main character and a basic scenario or setting to act as the basis of the story. Ask one person in each group to suggest an opening to the story. Encourage them to think creatively and speak their thoughts out loud to the group. The group should note down a summary of this opening. Alternatively, they could add their ideas Activity Sheet 2.1.8. The other members of the group should then take it in turns to contribute to the development of the plot, one episode at a time. They should try to make their suggestions as entertaining as possible. The rest of the group should note down the ideas under relevant headings such as 'part 1', 'part 2' or continue to complete Activity Sheet 2.1.8. After each student in the group has contributed, the group should discuss how to conclude the narrative they have created. They should work together to come-up with two possible endings. The narratives should then be presented to the class. The class should vote for the most appropriate ending to each narrative from the options provided. They should be given the opportunity to provide reasons for their views.

- Go through the features of what makes an accurate piece of writing using the features listed in the Student Book on page 146. You could use Presentation 2.1.2 to present these points on the whiteboard. Hand out Activity Sheet 2.1.2 or Activity 2.1.3, which both provide exemplar pieces of writing, and ask students to correct them and suggest improvements.

- Use Interactive 2.1.1 to help students read and engage with a series of examiner's comments, which link to example pieces of creative writing. Students can use the activity to link each comment to the relevant part of the student response on screen. You could display this interactive on the whiteboard and carry out the activity as a class.

A-A* students should...

- carefully select their content to firmly engage the reader's interest
- produce well-crafted and structured writing, using a variety of sentence structures and a wide range of vocabulary to achieve particular effects
- organize their material into effective, controlled paragraphs
- use accurate punctuation for deliberate effects and spell virtually all words correctly, including complex, irregular words
- make confident and purposeful use of tense changes.

C-B students should...

- produce relevant, coherent and engaging content using varied sentence lengths and structures
- organize their writing in an appropriate form using paragraphs
- produce effective, simple, compound and complex sentences using a range of vocabulary
- use punctuation effectively and spell most words correctly
- demonstrate a clear understanding and control of tense agreement.

E-D students should...

- produce relevant content that attempts to interest the reader
- use paragraphs logically to group ideas together and to lend some order to their writing
- choose certain words to create effects and spell the majority of simple words correctly
- show some control of a range of punctuation, including the punctuation of direct speech
- demonstrate some understanding and control of tense agreement.

Chapter 2.1b Creative Writing
How to teach GCSE English Unit 3 Section B

AO3

- Write clearly, effectively and imaginatively, using and adapting forms and selecting vocabulary appropriate to task and purpose in ways which engage the reader.
- Organize information and ideas into structured and sequenced sentences, paragraphs and whole texts, using a variety of linguistic and structural features to support cohesion and overall coherence.
- Use a range of sentence structures for clarity, purpose and effect, with accurate punctuation and spelling.

Introduction to the Controlled Assessment

Unit 3 is assessed through Controlled Assessment, which replaces traditional GCSE coursework. Unlike the examined units, it is not split into Foundation and Higher tier papers.

For Section B, students are expected to submit two pieces of narrative writing; one piece must be written from a first-person perspective and one piece must be written in the third person. WJEC will supply these tasks and they will be replaced every year. Responses must be in written form.

During the research and planning stage of the assessment, students may work under informal supervision and may refer to resources and stimulus materials relevant to their chosen tasks. The final pieces of writing must then be completed under controlled conditions in no more than two hours.

The time available for the final writing session may be split across shorter sessions. Students must hand their work in at the end of each session and this should be locked away until the next session begins.

Example writing tasks

Students will be asked to complete one first-person and one third-person narrative writing task.

First-person tasks may include:

- Write about an occasion when you…
- Recount an experience where you…
- Write about a situation in which you…
- Write about an incident which taught you…

Third-person tasks will require students to imagine a situation in which something happens to one or more characters. Students may write a narrative response to an evocative title such as: *The Dare*, *The Broken Promise*, *The Rebel* or *The Survivor*.

Key ideas

- Narrative writing is an account of connective events (key word = control).
- Features of good narrative writing:
  - well-judged plot and characters
  - good beginning and appropriate ending
  - purposeful and well-paced
  - paragraphs varied in length with appropriate connectives
  - the reader's interest is held.

- First-person writing is written from the 'I' or 'we' perspective; third-person writing is from the 'he', 'she' or 'they' perspective.
- Features of accurate writing:
  - sentences are varied and controlled
  - punctuation is used to clarify meaning and create effects
  - spelling of both simple and complex vocabulary is correct
  - grammar is used confidently and purposefully.

Ideas for starters and plenaries

- Write the opening sentence of a story on the board. Working in pairs or small groups students should create a paragraph to follow this opening and write it down. Feed back the responses to the class and discuss in what direction each group took the narrative. Which was the most effective/interesting?

- Read students the extracts on page 136 of the Student Book and ask them to come up with paragraphs of bad 'genre' writing of their own.

- Interactive 2.1.2 contains a selection of pieces of narrative writing together with related comments from an examiner. Ask students to 'mark' each piece of writing by matching the comments to the relevant section of each example response. After they have completed the activity ask them to write a list of five tips on how to create a successful piece of narrative writing, based on what they have learnt from the examiner's comments.

- Watch clips of the last few minutes of two popular films. If necessary, give a brief summary of what each film is about, what has happened in the immediate lead-up to the final scenes and who the key characters are. Ask students to comment on how they feel about each ending. What do they think works well about the ending? What is disappointing about it? What techniques does the scriptwriter/director use to signal that this is the conclusion of the narrative? Does the ending tie everything up neatly or leave some questions unanswered? Explain that when writing a conclusion to their own narratives, students will have to make similar choices.

- Ask students to work in pairs to write a 'cliff-hanger' sentence and read it to the class. Discuss how each team has created suspense. Pairs then swap sentences with another pair and write the following line (the aftermath/next day/next moment). What do the writers of the cliff-hangers think about the subsequent sentences?

Lesson ideas

- Ask students to look closely at the examples of 'genre writing' on page 136 of the Student Book and create a list of the faults and failings of each one. Students should use their list of points to create a 'What to avoid' guide for writing a successful narrative.

- Ask students to read the student response at the top of page 134. This could be a response to a descriptive writing task or a narrative writing task. Either way, it is very well structured. What is most effective about the way the writer has chosen to organize this piece of writing? Discuss how the organization of the text helps to build a feeling of suspense and anticipation as well as a convincing sense of movement. Ask students to re-arrange the sentences from this extract in order to create a passage with a different focus. Students could use Activity Sheet 2.1.9 to cut up and re-arrange the content of this extract.

- Having looked at the extract on page 134, students could analyse the longer response that appears under Point 3 on page 138. What techniques has this writer used to structure this part of the narrative? Students could attempt the question that relates to this extract on page 138. For further work on using structure for effect, students could attempt Interactive 2.1.4 either in groups or as a class. This interactive provides a sequencing activity where students can practise re-arranging an extract from a student response to create particular effects.

- Go through the features of good narrative writing using the responses in the Student Book as exemplars. Students can build their confidence in incorporating these features into their own writing through attempting the activities on pages 137–138. Use Activity Sheet 2.1.5 to allow students to put their skills to the test. This activity sheet includes a badly-structured narrative in need of a makeover.

- Encourage students to practice planning an appropriate level of content by considering the three example tasks at the bottom of page 137 and the example tasks on page 147. Explain the importance of considering the time available for the final assessment (one hour for each piece of writing) and how this is likely to impact upon the type of narrative that they will be able to write. It is important that students create a plot that is manageable in terms of length and complexity and also create a sensible number of characters. For each task title, ask students to suggest a suitable story-line and a brief profile of up to four characters that they might include. Once students have done this, ask them to swap their work with a partner to assess whether the outline and character profiles are fitting to the time available and the demands of the task.

- Discuss what makes an accurate piece of narrative writing using the features listed in the Student Book on page 146. You could use Presentation 2.1.2 to present these points on the whiteboard. Ask students to use Activity Sheet 2.1.4 to correct a selection of sample responses in line with the points discussed.

- Discuss the features of autobiographical writing, with reference to page 142 of the Student Book. How is the process of planning and writing a piece of autobiographical writing likely to differ from other forms of narrative writing? How is it likely to be similar? Draw out points such as writing from a first-person perspective, selecting events to focus on, structuring the narrative and looking back on events that have occurred in the past.

- Ask a student or a group of students to read the example response on pages 142 and 143 of the Student Book. How well does this fit the genre of autobiographical writing? What works well about it? Highlight factors such as the writer's willingness to express his or her feelings and the way he or she successfully conveys a sense of emotional involvement with the people and events described. Discuss how the writer selects and presents events, and sets this into the wider context of his or her life. This piece of writing has quite a reflective tone, how is this achieved? How does the writer balance his or her feelings at the time with his or her opinions and feelings in retrospect?

- Establish the differences between first- and third-person narrative writing with reference to page 144 of the Student Book. Students could attempt Interactive 2.1.3 to consolidate their knowledge. What are the strengths and weaknesses of each style of writing? What can and cannot be expressed through each perspective? Students could practise using each style of writing by attempting the activities on page 145.

A-A* students should...

- produce original and imaginative writing with a well-constructed plot and effective characterization
- organize their writing to successfully control the pace and progression of the narrative
- use a wide range of ambitious but appropriate vocabulary to convey precise meaning
- use a variety of sentences and accurate punctuation to create particular effects
- spell all words correctly, including complex, irregular words
- show confident and purposeful control of tense.

C-B students should...

- produce controlled and coherent writing with a structured plot and convincing characterization
- organize their narrative, so that it has shape, pace and detail
- use a range of sentences and punctuation accurately and sometimes to create specific effects
- use a range of vocabulary for effect or to convey precise meaning
- spell most words, including irregular words, correctly
- make accurate use of tense.

E-D students should...

- write a developed narrative to engage the reader with some control of plot and characterization
- structure their writing logically using paragraphs and write an appropriate beginning and conclusion
- use a mixture of compound and simple sentences and appropriate punctuation
- use some range of vocabulary, sometimes to create precise meaning
- use punctuation that is usually accurate, spell most simple words correctly and show general control of tense.

Chapter 2.2a Information and Ideas
How to teach GCSE English Language Unit 2

AO4

- Write to communicate clearly, effectively and imaginatively, using and adapting forms and selecting vocabulary appropriate to task and purpose in ways which engage the reader.
- Organize information and ideas into structured and sequenced sentences, paragraphs and whole texts, using a variety of linguistic and structural features to support cohesion and overall coherence.
- Use a range of sentence structures for clarity, purpose and effect, with accurate punctuation and spelling.

Introduction to the exam

This unit will be assessed by an exam that will last one hour in total. The exam will consist of two tasks, which will test transactional writing. Each task will be worth a total of 20 marks, so students are advised to spend an equal amount of time on each one. Across tasks, students may be asked to adapt their writing to a number of forms, such as a letter, a magazine article, a leaflet or a review. Whatever text they are asked to write, they will be given enough information in the question to allow them to identify the relevant audience and purpose of each text.

The exam will be separated into Foundation tier and Higher tier papers.

Example writing tasks

Students will be asked to complete two writing tasks. Each task will set-up a basic scenario, which will enable students to identify the relevant purpose and audience of the piece of writing. It will also specify what form of writing is required. For example:

- You have to give a talk to… with the title… Write what you would say.
- A company that… is looking to recruit a… Write your letter of application.
- You are a member of… which would like to inform… Write an article for a magazine.
- You have been asked by… to give your opinion on… Write your review.

Key ideas

- Transactional writing is 'real-life' writing.
- Key questions to consider when planning a piece of writing:
  - What is the purpose?
  - Who is the audience?
  - What is the format?
- Reports are written in an impersonal style, are usually aimed at a particular leader or governing body and provide conclusions and recommendations at the end.
- Formal letters include the sender and recipients address at the top, they are written in Standard English and they begin and end with an appropriate opening and signing off (Dear…/Yours…).
- Articles appear in newspapers and magazines, are written to interest the reader and often convey a particular point of view.
- Reviews convey a personal opinion about something the writer has experienced and aim to convince the reader to adopt the same opinion as the writer.
- Speeches can be formal or informal but should always be given in Standard English.
- Leaflets are short promotional texts aimed at attracting the reader's interest.

Key ideas (continued...)

- Writing with accuracy:

  ◆ spelling – pay attention to homophones, plurals, double consonants, prefixes, suffixes and silent letters

  ◆ grammar – ensure that expression is presented correctly and verb tenses, prepositions, pronouns and conjunctions are used appropriately.

  ◆ punctuation – sentence structure and punctuation are intrinsically linked, so sentences should be carefully constructed and punctuated appropriately.

Ideas for starters and plenaries

- Students could use pages 155 to 157 of the Student Book to familiarize themselves with the features of reports, letters, articles, reviews, speeches and leaflets and then attempt Interactive 2.2.5 to test their awareness of what stylistic features are appropriate to each form.

- Find two examples of speeches online and play extracts from these speeches to the class. The speeches could focus on any type of issue. Ask students to suggest what they think the purpose is for each speech, and who the target audience might be in each case. What characteristics are common between the examples? Which techniques are similar? Which are effective? Then, display Presentation 2.2.7 on the whiteboard and ask a member of the class to read the speech included. You could give them a printed copy to read from using Activity Sheet 2.2.6. What initial thoughts do students have in response to this speech? Display the final screen of Presentation 2.2.7 and read the examiner's comments. Highlight the examiner's point that the response does not seem to be particularly well-suited to the form required. How could the writer make the response look and work more like a speech? Direct students to page 157 of the Student Book for points to consider.

- Display Presentation 2.2.4 on the whiteboard. Ask a student to read the first unpunctuated extract aloud. Ask the class to suggest where the full stops should go. If possible, mark their suggestions on the whiteboard. Ask the same student to read out the corrected extract. Which version was better and why? You can repeat the activity with slide 2 and slide 3, which both provide further extracts to work with.

- Presentation 2.2.6 contains an example of a leaflet that has been written to warn children about the dangers of fireworks. Display the presentation on the whiteboard and ask students to read part of it. What is the initial reaction to the leaflet? Consider purpose, audience and format. Do students think that this leaflet conveys an effective warning? How well does it suit the target audience? Is the content and style suitable for a leaflet format? Reveal the examiner's comment on the second slide of the presentation and highlight the point that the examiner makes about tone. How could the writer improve the tone of the leaflet? What other approaches could a writer take to influence this type of audience?

- Bring in a selection of newspapers and magazines or ask students to bring in examples from home. Go over the features of articles on page 156 of the Student Book and then hand out the magazines and newspapers to students. Students could work in small groups or in pairs. Ask students to scan through the material they have to find examples of articles, and in particular the features mentioned on page 156. They could perhaps compile examples on an A2 piece of paper and annotate them. They should also highlight any other common features they notice.

Lesson ideas

- Discuss the key questions to consider when creating a piece of transactional writing as covered on page 154 of the Student Book. You could display these questions on the whiteboard using Presentation 2.2.1. Display the fourth screen of the presentation, which includes a number of example forms of writing such as a letter, an article and a review. For each one, ask students to think of as many different types of audience, or purposes as they can, that might be relevant to this type of text.

- Discuss the features of letters listed on page 155 of the Student Book. Ask students to comment on why these features are important and how they relate to the purpose of letter-writing. Then hand out Activity Sheet 2.2.1, which contains examples of two letters and ask students to identify the strengths and weaknesses of each one.

- Ask students to work in pairs to determine three reasons why using paragraphs improves the quality of writing. Ask some of the pairs to feed back and create a list of reasons on the whiteboard. For example, paragraphs can be used to organize information, to divide content into more readable chunks and to help structure an argument. Varying paragraphs can also be used to create impact or highlight important information. Give each student a copy of Activity Sheet 2.2.2 which contains a letter that has been written without paragraphs. Ask students, in their pairs, to mark where the paragraphs should appear in the text.

- Provide students with a copy of Activity Sheet 2.2.7, which contains an example of a letter, which lacks carefully thought-out counter-arguments. Working in pairs, students should consider where the writer's argument falls down. What arguments can they think of to challenge the writer's point of view? Ask them to list as many ideas as they can think of and then pick their three strongest points. Once they have done this, ask students to work independently to re-draft the letter, taking into account their three alternative viewpoints and offering a convincing counter-argument for each one.

- Make the point that letters are likely to have more impact on the reader if the content is organized in a logical and structured way. Ask students for ideas about how they might go about structuring a letter. What kind of things should they include at the start of the letter? What kind of things should be mentioned at the end? If the writer wishes to cover multiple topics, how should he or she set these topics out? How might planning help a writer to better structure a letter?

- Ask students to carry out a sequencing exercise using Interactive 2.2.2. The interactive includes a top-grade sample student response in the form of a letter. At the end of the activity students can read the examiner's comments on the response. Alternatively, Interactive 2.2.3 provides an activity where students must correctly sequence a piece of writing written in the form of a leaflet. Interactive 2.2.4 follows the some format but includes an example of a speech.

- An important part of creating any piece of persuasive writing is identifying and presenting counter-arguments. Ask students to look at the section headed 'Writing process' on pages 160 and 161 of the Student Book. In particular look closely at the three paragraphs at the bottom of page 160 and the final paragraph on page 161. Ask students to pick one of the sample tasks given on page 160 and decide whether they are going to write for or against the given topic.

- If the student decides to write 'for' one of the topics on page 160, then ask them to think of three arguments against the topic that they must counter. How will they counter these arguments? If they decide to write 'against' the topic, then ask them to think of three arguments for the topic that they must counter. Again, ask them to make notes on how they would counter these arguments. Presentation 2.2.5 provides support for this with suggested arguments for and against each topic. Stress that the key to writing a persuasive argument is to think carefully about counter-arguments and build these into the response.

- Go through the features of articles covered on page 156 of the Student Book. Then display Presentations 2.2.2 on the whiteboard, which contains an article on smoking. Read the article with the class and ask them to identify what they find effective about it and what could be improved. If possible, annotate the article on the board with their ideas.

- Discuss the features of reports listed on page 155 of the Student Book and ask students to give alternative examples of how each feature might appear in a report. Instead of 'Report on the eating habits of school children' for example, a report could be entitled 'Report on the dangers of using mobile phones'. Ask for suggestions on what is meant by an 'impersonal style'. Using Activity Sheet 2.2.3, ask students to correct the written style of the example report provided.

- Using Activity Sheet 2.2.4 and the examples of leaflet-writing that appear on pages 167 to 169 of the Student Book, ask students to identify the weaknesses of each extract and then re-write a better version of each. Activity Sheet 2.2.5 includes further examples of letter-writing that can be used for a similar activity. Remind students that they can use the checklists provided on pages 174–175 of the Student Book to assess the extracts and to identify ways to improve them.

A-A* students should...

- write content that is well-judged and firmly engages the reader's interest
- use an appropriate form with distinctive structural and stylistic features
- create a well-crafted piece of writing making use of varied sentences and paragraphs and an ambitious but appropriate range of vocabulary
- use punctuation accurately to vary the pace of the writing, to clarify meaning and to create deliberate effects
- spell virtually all words, including complex, irregular words, correctly
- use tense confidently and with purpose.

C-B students should...

- write content that is relevant and coherent and engages the reader's interest
- use an appropriate form and structure and write effectively using paragraphs
- employ a range of vocabulary, chosen to either convey precise meaning or create effects
- use a range of sentences to achieve particular effects and use punctuation accurately
- spell most words, including irregular words, correctly and show control of tense agreement.

E-D students should...

- write content that is relevant and attempts to interest the reader
- use paragraphs logically to structure and sequence their writing and adopt a form that is largely appropriate to the task
- use a range of vocabulary, sometimes chosen to convey precise meaning or create specific effects
- make use of a variety of compound and complex sentences and spell most simple words correctly
- show general control of tense agreement.

Chapter 2.2b Information and Ideas
How to teach GCSE English Unit 2

- Write to communicate clearly, effectively and imaginatively, using and adapting forms and selecting vocabulary appropriate to task and purpose in ways which engage the reader.
- Organize information and ideas into structured and sequenced sentences, paragraphs and whole texts, using a variety of linguistic and structural features to support cohesion and overall coherence.
- Use a range of sentence structures for clarity, purpose and effect, with accurate punctuation and spelling.

Introduction to the exam

This unit will be assessed by an exam that will last one hour in total. The exam will consist of two tasks, which will test transactional writing. Each task will be worth a total of 20 marks, so students are advised to spend an equal amount of time on each one. Across tasks, students may be asked to adapt their writing to a number of forms, such as a letter, a magazine article, a leaflet or a review. Whatever text they are asked to write, they will be given enough information in the question to allow them to identify the relevant audience and purpose of each text.

The exam will be separated into Foundation tier and Higher tier papers.

Example writing tasks

Students will be asked to complete two writing tasks. Each task will set-up a basic scenario, which will enable students to identify the relevant purpose and audience of the piece of writing. It will also specify what form of writing is required. For example:

- You have to give a talk to… with the title… Write what you would say.
- A company that… is looking to recruit a… Write your letter of application.
- You are a member of… which would like to inform… Write an article for a magazine.
- You have been asked by… to give your opinion on… Write your review.

Key ideas

- Transactional writing is 'real-life' writing.
- Key questions to consider when planning a piece of writing:
  - What is the purpose?
  - Who is the audience?
  - What is the format?
- Reports are written in an impersonal style, are usually aimed at a particular leader or governing body and provide conclusions and recommendations at the end.
- Formal letters include the addresses of the sender and recipient at the top, they are written in Standard English and they begin and end with an appropriate opening and signing off (Dear…/Yours…).
- Articles appear in newspapers and magazines, are written to interest the reader and often convey a particular point of view.
- Reviews convey a personal opinion about an object, place or experience and aim to convince the reader to adopt the same opinion as the writer.
- Speeches can be formal or informal but should always be given in Standard English.
- Leaflets are short promotional texts aimed at attracting the reader's interest.

Key ideas (continued...)

- Writing with accuracy:
  - spelling – pay attention to homophones, plurals, double consonants, prefixes, suffixes and silent letters

  - grammar – ensure that expression is presented correctly and verb tenses, prepositions, pronouns

and conjunctions are used appropriately.

- punctuation – sentence structure and punctuation are intrinsically linked, so sentences should be carefully constructed and punctuated appropriately.

Ideas for starters and plenaries

- Students could use pages 155 to 157 of the Student Book to familiarize themselves with the features of reports, letters, articles, reviews, speeches and leaflets and then attempt Interactive 2.2.5 to test their awareness of what stylistic features are appropriate to each form.

- Find two examples of speeches online and play extracts from these speeches to the class. The speeches could focus on any type of issue. Ask students to suggest what they think the purpose is for each speech, and who the target audience might be in each case. What characteristics are common between the examples? Which techniques are similar? Which are effective? Then, display Presentation 2.2.7 on the whiteboard and ask a member of the class to read the speech included. You could give them a printed copy to read from using Activity Sheet 2.2.6. What initial thoughts do students have in response to this speech? Display the final screen of Presentation 2.2.7 and read the examiner's comments. Highlight the examiner's point that the response does not seem to be particularly well-suited to the form required. How could the writer make the response look and work more like a speech? Direct students to page 157 of the Student Book for points to consider.

- Ask students to work in pairs and for each type of text listed on page 154 ask them to suggest two possible reasons why somebody might like to create a text like this. For example, someone might write a letter to a supermarket to complain about the lack of fair trade goods on sale or someone might write a letter to a company to apply for a job. Try to encourage specific suggestions.

- Display Interactive 2.2.1 on the whiteboard and ask students to link each extract to the relevant format.

- Presentation 2.2.6 contains an example of a leaflet that has been written to warn children about the dangers of fireworks. Display the presentation on the whiteboard and ask students to read part of it. What is the initial reaction to the leaflet? Consider purpose, audience and format. Do students think that this leaflet conveys an effective warning? How well does it suit the target audience? Is the content and style suitable for a leaflet format? Reveal the examiner's comment on the second slide of the presentation and highlight the point that the examiner makes about tone. How could the writer improve the tone of the leaflet? What other approaches could a writer take to influence this type of audience?

- Bring in a selection of newspapers and magazines or ask students to bring in examples from home. Go over the features of articles on page 156 of the Student Book and then hand out the magazines and newspapers to students. Students could work in small groups or in pairs. Ask students to scan through the material they have to find examples of articles, and in particular the features mentioned on page 156. They could perhaps compile examples on an A2 piece of paper and annotate them. They should also highlight any other common features they notice.

Lesson ideas

- Discuss the features of letters listed on page 155 of the Student Book. Ask students to comment on why these features are important and how they relate to the purpose of letter-writing. Then hand out Activity Sheet 2.2.1, which contains examples of two letters and ask students to identify the strengths and weaknesses of each one.

- Ask students to work in pairs to determine three reasons why using paragraphs improves the quality of writing. Ask some of the pairs to feed back and create a list of top reasons on the whiteboard. For example, paragraphs can be used to organize information, to divide content into more readable chunks and to help structure an argument. Varying paragraphs can also be used to create impact or highlight important information. Give each student a copy of Activity Sheet 2.2.2 which contains a letter that has been written without paragraphs. Ask students, in their pairs, to mark where the paragraphs should appear in the text.

- Make the point that letters are likely to have more impact on the reader if the content is organized in a logical and structured way. Ask students for ideas about how they might go about structuring a letter. What kind of things should they include at the start of the letter? What should be mentioned at the end? If the writer wishes to cover multiple topics, how should he or she set these topics out? How might planning help a writer to better structure a letter?

- Provide students with a copy of Activity Sheet 2.2.7, which contains an example of a letter, which lacks carefully thought-out counter-arguments. Working in pairs, students should consider where the writer's argument falls down. What arguments can they think of to challenge the writer's point of view? Ask them to list as many ideas as they can think of and then pick their three strongest points. Once they have done this, ask students to work independently to re-draft the letter, taking into account their three alternative viewpoints and offering a convincing counter-argument for each one.

- Ask students to carry out a sequencing exercise using Interactive 2.2.2. The interactive includes a top-grade sample student response in the form of a letter. At the end of the activity students can read the examiner's comments on the response. Alternatively, Interactive 2.2.3 provides an activity where students must correctly sequence a piece of writing written in the form of a leaflet. Interactive 2.2.4 follows the same format but includes an example of a speech.

- An important part of creating any piece of persuasive writing is identifying and presenting counter-arguments. Ask students to look at the section headed 'Writing process' on pages 160 and 161 of the Student Book. In particular look closely at the three paragraphs at the bottom of page 160 and the final paragraph on page 161. Ask students to pick one of the sample tasks given on page 160 and decide whether they are going to write for or against the given topic.

- If the student decides to write 'for' one of the topics on page 160, then ask them to think of three arguments against the topic that they must counter. How will they counter these arguments? If they decide to write 'against' the topic, then ask them to think of three arguments for the topic that they must counter. Again, ask them to make notes on how they would counter these arguments. Presentation 2.2.5 provides support for this with suggested arguments for and against each topic. Stress that the key to writing a persuasive argument is to think carefully about counter-arguments and build these into the response.

- Go through the features of articles covered on page 156 of the Student Book. Then display Presentation 2.2.3 on the whiteboard, which contains an article on smoking. Read the article with the class and ask students to identify what they find effective about it and what could be improved. If possible, annotate the article on the board with their ideas.

- Discuss the features of reports listed on page 155 of the Student Book and ask students to give alternative examples of how each feature might appear in a report. Instead of 'Report on the eating habits of school children' for example, a report could be entitled 'Report on the dangers of mobile phone use'. Ask for suggestions on what is meant by an 'impersonal style'. Using Activity Sheet 2.2.3, ask students to correct the written style of the example report provided.

- Using Activity Sheet 2.2.4 and the examples of leaflet-writing that appear on page 167 to 169 of the Student Book, ask students to identify the weaknesses of each extract and then re-write a better version of each. Activity Sheet 2.2.5 includes further examples of letter-writing that can be used for a similar activity. Remind students that they can use the checklists provided on pages 174–175 of the Student Book to assess the extracts and to identify ways to improve them.

A-A* students should...

- write content that is well-judged and firmly engages the reader's interest
- use an appropriate form with distinctive structural or stylistic features
- create a well-crafted piece of writing making use of varied sentences and paragraphs and an ambitious but appropriate range of vocabulary
- use punctuation accurately to vary the pace of the writing, to clarify meaning and to create deliberate effects
- spell virtually all words, including complex, irregular words, correctly
- use tense confidently and with purpose.

C-B students should...

- write content that is relevant and coherent and engages the reader's interest
- use an appropriate form and structure and write effectively using paragraphs
- employ a range of vocabulary, chosen to either convey precise meaning or create effects
- use a range of sentences to achieve particular effects and use punctuation accurately
- spell most words, including irregular words, correctly and show control of tense agreement.

E-D students should...

- write content that is relevant and attempts to interest the reader
- use paragraphs logically to structure and sequence their writing, and adopt a form that is largely appropriate to the task
- use a range of vocabulary, sometimes chosen to convey precise meaning or create specific effects
- make use of a variety of compound and complex sentences and spell most simple words correctly
- show general control of tense agreement.

Chapter 3.1a Speaking and Listening
How to teach GCSE English Language Unit 4 Section A

> **AO1**
> - Speak to communicate clearly and purposefully; structure and sustain talk, adapting it to different situations and audiences; use Standard English and a variety of techniques as appropriate.
> - Listen and respond to speakers' ideas, perspectives and how they construct and express their meanings.
> - Interact with others, shaping meanings through suggestions, comments and questions and drawing ideas together.
> - Create and sustain different roles.

Introduction to the Controlled Assessment

Unit 4 is assessed by Controlled Assessment. The assessment is divided into two sections, the first of which will test speaking and listening. For this part of the assessment students are required to complete at least three speaking and listening tasks. The tasks might be based on texts or themes that students have covered elsewhere in the course and can involve both scripted and improvised work. The three tasks must cover the following areas:

- communicating and adapting language
- interacting and responding
- creating and sustaining roles.

WJEC will provide exemplar tasks, but centres can design their own tasks to best suit the needs of students. Centres must ensure that two of the tasks are of a functional nature. Across the three tasks, students must be assessed on their ability to:

- present and listen to information and ideas
- respond appropriately to questions and views of others
- make a range of effective contributions
- reflect and comment critically on their own and other's use of language
- participate in a range of real-life contexts beyond the classroom and adapt talk appropriately to situation and audience
- select and use a range of dramatic techniques and creative approaches to explore ideas, texts and issues.

Students must complete their final speaking and listening tasks under formal supervision. During the research and planning stage of the assessment, students may work under limited supervision and carry out research to inform the subject-matter of their speaking and listening tasks.

While students must demonstrate that they can work with others during discussion-based and role-play tasks, it is also important that each candidate makes a sufficient contribution to allow them to be assessed individually.

Tasks should be assessed by the teacher, either at the time of the response or upon reviewing a visual recording of the task.

Example speaking and listening tasks

Example tasks will be provided by WJEC, but these can be adapted to suit particular contexts. The list below, suggests some possible tasks that would be suitable for this Controlled Assessment:

Communicating and adapting language

- Give an account of a personal experience.
- Present an argument in favour of or against a local issue.
- Lead a challenging discussion, adapting language accordingly.

Interacting and responding

- Discussion of a familiar topic such as the legal driving age.
- Discussion of a less familiar topic such as a current news item or local issue.
- Discussion arising from reading of a literary text, such as an interpretation of character.
- Sustained discussion of a more complex topic such as age discrimination.

Creating and sustaining roles

- Create a role in a familiar situation such as in a school or home environment.
- Develop and sustain a role in a less familiar situation such as in a shop or in an office environment.
- Create an improvisation as a pair or group based on one of the texts studied.
- Create a complex character in a challenging role in an unfamiliar environment such as a board meeting or a public demonstration.

Key ideas

- The speaking and listening assessment will assess:
  - a talk given in the classroom
  - participation in a group discussion
  - participation in a role-play of an everyday situation.
- The best speaking and listening work shows a clear awareness of the audience and purpose.
- Listening skills are just as important as speaking skills in this unit.
- Notes are allowed, but it is important not to simply read from them.
- Planning for speaking and listening tasks might include:
  - researching the topic or subject-matter of the talk/discussion/presentation
  - thinking of possible counter-arguments in advance of the discussion in order to formulate a convincing response to these points
  - selecting interesting, bite-size facts that can be used to back-up points in the talk or discussion.
- When planning to speak in role, you should select an appropriate tone, focus and range of vocabulary to suit the character you are going to play.

- Tips for speaking:
  - remain focused on the topic being discussed
  - establish eye contact with the audience
  - make at least one relevant contribution in a discussion
  - make a comment early to help dispel nerves
  - do not interrupt other speakers
  - be polite
  - do not monopolize the discussion
  - be enthusiastic
  - make use of positive body language.
- Tips for listening:
  - always listen to what is said
  - do not yawn or look bored
  - face speakers and give them full attention
  - use positive body language
  - encourage nervous speakers.

> **Key ideas (continued...)**
>
> - Tips for interacting with your audience:
>   - use visual/multimedia aids
>   - consider including a practical demonstration
>   - consider the location of the talk/discussion
>   - consider using direct questioning
>   - invite questions at the end of a talk/presentation.

Ideas for starters and plenaries

- Display Presentation 3.1.1, which contains a slideshow of a random selection of images. For each slide, ask students to work in pairs to suggest possible topics for a talk, which relate to the image. Encourage students to be as creative as they like with their suggestions. The first slide gives some tips on choosing a suitable format for the talk. This is also covered in pages 180–181 of the Student Book. Remind students that the format of their speech could be an account of a personal experience, an argument for or against a local issue, a speech about a challenging topic or a talk that relates to a novel, poem or drama text that they have read for another part of their course.

- In pairs, students should work out the detailed views of two people with opposite beliefs. Students should collaborate in developing their material, using arguments and counter-arguments to make a persuasive case for each of the individuals: 1a. A parent who believes in the strict upbringing of children, 1b. A parent who believes in giving freedom of expression to children, 2a. A head teacher who believes in old-fashioned values of discipline and order, 2b. A head teacher who believes in children making their own decisions about their learning, 3a. A boss of a company who creates strict work conditions for his/her employees, 3b. A boss of a company who encourages flexible and independent thinking in his/her employees. Each student will then take one of the individuals and make an informal, persuasive contribution for a radio phone-in on the topic of 'discipline'. They could record their responses using the Record and Playback software for this activity on the OxBox, (Record and Playback 3.1.5).

- Ask students to carry out the self-assessment exercise on page 179 of the Student Book. A version of this is provided on Activity Sheet 3.1.8 with spaces for students to write in their responses. Ask students to think about how they could improve their speaking and listening skills and set themselves three targets to focus on, as they progress through the course. These could be specific such as, 'try not to rush what I say when I speak' or more general such as 'pay more attention to other speakers in speaking and listening work'. Students could use the Examiner's Tip at the bottom of page 179 for ideas about how they could improve their performance in this area.

- Think about audience. How can speakers adapt what they say and how they speak to appeal to particular listeners? Display Presentation 3.1.4, which contains images representing different audiences. What is it possible to determine about the audience from each image? What factors would a speaker need to take into account when speaking to this kind of audience? How could they adapt their tone, vocabulary and body language to communicate effectively in this situation? What should they avoid doing and why? As a class, build a list of variable speaking and listening techniques that depend on the audience.

Lesson ideas

- Discuss what is required when giving an account of a personal experience as the subject matter of a talk. Refer students to page 180 of the Student Book and ask them to work in pairs to plan a narrative suitable for delivery as a talk. Each member of the pair should plan his or her own presentation, taking into account feedback from his or her partner. Presentation 3.1.2 provides a series of tips that can be displayed to assist students with this task. Students can then deliver their talk to the class or to a group of other pairs. They could also make a recording of their talk using the Record and Playback software for this activity on the OxBox (Record and Playback 3.1.1).

● Students should read the section headed 'Present an argument for or against a local issue' on page 180 of the Student Book and the section entitled 'Lead a challenging discussion, adapting language accordingly' on page 181. Students should select a topic and then work in pairs to plan a talk for it. Students should carry out their planning in pairs but should each produce a plan for a different talk. Once they have planned their speech, they could deliver it to the class or a smaller group of students. Alternatively, they could record it using the Record and Playback software on the OxBox, (Record and Playback 3.1.2). This will guide students through the talk in steps and give them a chance to review and re-record sections of the talk that they are unhappy with. Students may work on the same topic or both focus on different ones. Presentation 3.1.3 provides tips to help students plan and deliver their talks.

● Select a text that students are studying for another part of the course and create a list of related topics that students could use as the basis for a talk. Cut a sheet of A4 paper into eight pieces and write a topic on each piece. You could use Activity Sheet 3.1.1 for this. Place each card face-down on a table at the front of the class. Then, make a list of eight different types of audience and do the same thing. Arrange these cards face-down on another table in front of the class. You could use Activity Sheet 3.3.2 for this, which already includes eight different types of audience. This can be adapted as necessary to best suit the text. Divide the class into groups. Ask one of the students from each group to come up to the front of the class and pick one card from each table. They then read out the topic and the audience that they have selected. The group has one opportunity to veto this selection, if they wish. In which case, they must call out 'veto' and then the student at the front must select another two cards. Every student in the group must then plan their own individual talk based on the topic and audience chosen. They could refer to Activity Sheet 3.1.3 to help them plan their work.

● Alternatively, if students require greater support when planning their talk, they could attempt the activity suggested on page 181 of the Student Book. This activity allows students to present in groups, whilst still making an independent contribution adequate for assessment for this part of the unit. Students must participate in a 'Question Time' style activity based on a literary text they have studied. Speakers will make up a panel of four and the class will act as the audience. The speakers will be given a series of topics or exam questions in advance so that they can plan their responses. These topics could be decided by the class before the event of the talk and different members of the audience could be nominated to ask different questions. Each panel member should lead on a question, providing a full response. Other members of the panel will then have an opportunity to develop or qualify what the first speaker said. Possible questions are given on page 181 of the Student Book.

● Activity Sheet 3.1.4 provides support for a talk on a particular character from a literary text. Students could work in pairs to plan and develop a talk to suit this subject matter before delivering it to the class.

● Students could then take it in turns to record the talk based on a literary text using the Record and Playback software provided with the OxBox, (Record and Playback 3.1.3). A number of responses could then be selected at random from the finished recordings. These could be played to the class and students prompted to provide feedback.

- Explain how students are assessed on their ability to 'interact and respond' as part of the speaking and listening unit of their qualification. Refer to page 183 of the Student Book. Stress that the important thing about this part of the unit is for students to show that they can use speaking and listening skills effectively when working as part of a team. Ask students to work in groups of four or five to select a topic from the list provided on page 183 of the Student Book. Before students engage in discussion about the topic, ask them to think independently for a few minutes about the kind of points they would like to raise. Then ask the groups to get together and carry out a discussion. Following the discussion the group should work as a team to summarize the most important and interesting points raised, so that they can feed these points back to the class.

- For further practice students could set up a panel-based discussion similar to the format used for the party leader's debate in the run up to the 2010 general election. Students could watch clips from this three-part debate online to give them a sense of the format of this type of discussion. They could then refer to page 181 of the Student Book, which explains how to set-up a similar discussion. They could change the focus of the discussion from a literary text to a topical issue, for example: the smoking ban in pubs, arranged marriage or how famous sporting figures are treated by the media. Alternatively, each of the speakers could develop a 'policy' of their own that they would like to see introduced in response to a topical issue. They would then need to express their views and justify their policy in the light of questions from the audience. Activity Sheet 3.1.5 provides a customizable version of the 'Question Time' activity on page 181 that can be modified to focus on any topic. Activity Sheet 3.1.6 provides students with further support for planning this kind of discussion.

- Explain that as part of their speaking and listening assessment, students will be expected to show that they can create and sustain roles. Referring to page 186 of the Student Book, point out that this does not mean students are allowed to stick rigidly to a script. They will be expected to improvise to suit the circumstances of the assessment. This means that students need to be flexible in their roles so that they can adapt what they say and how they act according to what other speakers do during the assessment. Ask students to select a task from page 186 or 187 of the Student Book and develop a response in pairs. Students should decide on: the perspective they are each going to take in the dialogue, how they will convey a sense of character in each case and how they can use body language to enhance the performance. Students could use Record and Playback 3.1.4 to practise their dialogue and then either play a final version of the recording back to the class or perform it live.

- For further support for, and practice with, sustaining roles, students could attempt the scenario provided with Activity Sheet 3.1.7. This activity asks students to take on the role of a person applying for a job at a theme park. They have to prepare for, and take part in, an interview for this job. Students could use Record and Playback 3.1.6 to practise their response to this activity.

A-A* students should...

- speak effectively, highlighting the essential details when communicating a complex and demanding subject-matter
- use a sophisticated range of strategies to suit the context and purpose of the task
- use Standard English confidently and flexibly, employing a range of vocabulary and grammatical structures to best suit the purpose of the task
- listen with concentration throughout, using questions to supplement their understanding of what is said
- demonstrate the ability to influence the direction and content of the talk, through actively developing ideas and challenging assumptions
- encourage the participation of others, resolving differences and moving the talk towards a positive outcome
- create complex characters when speaking in role, sustaining a convincing persona through insightful choices and making full use of dramatic approaches
- demonstrate the ability to respond to complex issues and relationships, whilst in role, in varied formal and informal scenarios.

C-B students should...

- convey and interpret information confidently, emphasizing significant points and issues
- shape talk and non-verbal features to best suit the demands of particular contexts and purposes
- use Standard English appropriately and effectively
- respond thoughtfully and considerately to what they hear, challenging and developing ideas with appropriate questions
- help to structure the discussion by identifying useful outcomes and making purposeful contributions
- create a convincing character when speaking in role, using a range of well-selected verbal and non-verbal techniques
- respond with skill and sensitivity, whilst in role, in a range of situations exploring ideas, issues and relationships.

E-D students should...

- communicate information, viewpoints and feelings effectively
- adapt their talk to suit a variety of situations, using non-verbal features for impact
- use Standard English appropriately, using a range of vocabulary and sentence structures to achieve different purposes
- engage with what is heard through perceptive responses
- listen carefully and move discussions forward by engaging with the ideas of others and making relevant contributions
- use appropriate language choices and gestures to sustain a sense of character
- demonstrate an understanding of relationships and significant issues, whilst in character.

Chapter 3.1b Speaking and Listening
How to teach GCSE English Unit 4

AO1

- Speak to communicate clearly and purposefully; structure and sustain talk, adapting it to different situations and audiences; use Standard English and a variety of techniques as appropriate.
- Listen and respond to speakers' ideas, perspectives and how they construct and express their meanings.
- Interact with others, shaping meanings through suggestions, comments and questions and drawing ideas together.
- Create and sustain different roles.

Introduction to the Controlled Assessment

Unit 4 is assessed by Controlled Assessment. For this assessment students are required to complete at least three speaking and listening tasks. The tasks might be based on texts or themes that students have covered elsewhere in the course and can involve both scripted and improvised work. The three tasks must cover the following areas:

- communicating and adapting language
- interacting and responding
- creating and sustaining roles.

WJEC will provide exemplar tasks, but centres can design their own tasks to best suit the needs of students. Centres must ensure that two of the tasks are of a functional nature. Across the three tasks, students must be assessed on their ability to:

- present and listen to information and ideas
- respond appropriately to questions and views of others
- make a range of effective contributions
- reflect and comment critically on their own and other's use of language
- participate in a range of real-life contexts beyond the classroom and adapt talk appropriately to situation and audience
- select and use a range of dramatic techniques and creative approaches to explore ideas, texts and issues.

Students must complete their final speaking and listening tasks under formal supervision. During the research and planning stage of the assessment, students may work under limited supervision and carry out research to inform the subject-matter of their speaking and listening tasks.

While students must demonstrate that they can work with others during discussion-based and role-play tasks, it is also important that each candidate makes a sufficient contribution to allow them to be assessed individually.

Tasks should be assessed by the teacher, either at the time of the response or upon reviewing a visual recording of the task.

Example speaking and listening tasks

Example tasks will be provided by WJEC, but these can be adapted to suit particular contexts. The list below, suggests some possible tasks that would be suitable for this Controlled Assessment:

Communicating and adapting language

- Give an account of a personal experience.
- Present an argument in favour of or against a local issue.
- Lead a challenging discussion, adapting language accordingly.

Interacting and responding

- Discussion of a familiar topic such as using mobile phones in schools.
- Discussion of a less familiar topic such as a current news item or local issue.
- Discussion arising from reading of a literary text, such as an interpretation of character.
- Sustained discussion of a more complex topic such as freedom of speech.

Creating and sustaining roles

- Create a role in a familiar situation such as in a school or home environment.
- Develop and sustain a role in a less familiar situation such as in a shop or in an office environment.
- Create an improvisation as a pair or group based on one of the texts studied.
- Create a complex character in a challenging role in an unfamiliar environment such as a court room or press conference.

Key ideas

- The speaking and listening assessment will assess:
  - a talk given in the classroom
  - participation in a group discussion
  - participation in a role-play of an everyday situation.
- The best speaking and listening work shows a clear awareness of the audience and purpose.
- Listening skills are just as important as speaking skills in this unit.
- Notes are allowed, but it is important not to simply read from them.
- Planning for speaking and listening tasks might include:
  - researching the topic or subject-matter of the talk/discussion/presentation
  - thinking of possible counter-arguments in advance of the discussion in order to formulate a convincing response to these points
  - selecting interesting, bite-size facts that can be used to back-up points in the talk or discussion.
- When planning to speak in role, you should select an appropriate tone, focus and range of vocabulary to suit the character you are going to play.

- Tips for speaking:
  - remain focused on the topic being discussed
  - establish eye contact with the audience
  - make at least one relevant contribution in a discussion
  - make a comment early to help dispel nerves
  - do not interrupt other speakers
  - be polite
  - do not monopolize the discussion
  - be enthusiastic
  - make use of positive body language.
- Tips for listening:
  - always listen to what is said
  - do not yawn or look bored
  - face speakers and give them full attention
  - use positive body language
  - encourage nervous speakers.

> **Key ideas (continued...)**
>
> - Tips for interacting with you audience:
>   - use visual/multimedia aids
>   - consider including a practical demonstration
>   - consider the location of the talk/discussion
>   - consider using direct questioning
>   - invite questions at the end of a talk/presentation.

Ideas for starters and plenaries

- Display Presentation 3.1.1, which contains a slideshow of a random selection of images. For each slide, ask students to work in pairs to suggest possible topics for a talk, which relate to the image. Encourage students to be as creative as they like with their suggestions. The first slide gives some tips on choosing a suitable format for the talk. This is also covered in pages 180–181 of the Student Book. Remind students that the format of their speech could be an account of a personal experience, an argument for or against a local issue, a speech about a challenging topic or a talk that relates to a novel, poem or drama text that they have read for another part of their course.

- In pairs, students should work out the detailed views of two people with opposite beliefs. Students should collaborate in developing their material, using arguments and counter-arguments to make a persuasive case for each of the individuals: 1a. A parent who believes in the strict upbringing of children, 1b. A parent who believes in giving freedom of expression to children, 2a. A head teacher who believes in old-fashioned values of discipline and order, 2b. A head teacher who believes in children making their own decisions about their learning, 3a. A boss of a company who creates strict work conditions for his/her employees, 3b. A boss of a company who encourages flexible and independent thinking in his/her employees. Each student will then take one of the individuals and make an informal, persuasive contribution for a radio phone-in on the topic of 'discipline'. They could record their responses using the Record and Playback software for this activity on the OxBox, (Record and Playback 3.1.5).

- Ask students to carry out the self-assessment exercise on page 179 of the Student Book. A version of this is provided on Activity Sheet 3.1.8 with spaces for students to write in their responses. Ask students to think about how they could improve their speaking and listening skills and set themselves three targets to focus on, as they progress through the course. These could be specific such as, 'try not to rush what I say when I speak' or more general such as 'pay more attention to other speakers in speaking and listening work'. Students could use the Examiner's Tip at the bottom of page 179 for ideas about how they could improve their performance in this area.

- Think about audience. How can speakers adapt what they say and how they speak to appeal to particular listeners? Display Presentation 3.1.4, which contains images representing different audiences. What is it possible to determine about the audience from each image? What factors would a speaker need to take into account when speaking to this kind of audience? How could they adapt their tone, vocabulary and body language to communicate effectively in this situation? What should they avoid doing and why? As a class, build a list of variable speaking and listening techniques that depend on the audience.

Lesson ideas

- Discuss what is required when giving an account of a personal experience as the subject matter of a talk. Refer students to page 180 of the Student Book and ask them to work in pairs to plan a narrative suitable for delivery as a talk. Each member of the pair should plan his or her own presentation, taking into account feedback from his or her partner. Presentation 3.1.2 provides a series of tips that can be displayed to assist students with this task. Students can then deliver their talk to the class or to a group of other pairs. They could also make a recording of their talk using the Record and Playback software for this activity on the OxBox, (Record and Playback 3.1.1).

- Students should read the section headed 'Present an argument for or against a local issue' on page 180 of the Student Book and the section entitled 'Lead a challenging discussion, adapting language accordingly' on page 181. Students should select a topic and then work in pairs to plan a talk for it. Students should carry out their planning in pairs but should each produce a plan for a different talk. Once they have planned their speech, they could deliver it to the class or a smaller group of students. Alternatively, they could record it using the Record and Playback software on the OxBox, (Record and Playback 3.1.2). This will guide students through the talk in steps and give them a chance to review and re-record sections of the talk that they are unhappy with. Students may work on the same topic or both focus on different ones. Presentation 3.1.3 provides tips to help students plan and deliver their talks.

- Select a text that students are studying for another part of the course and create a list of related topics that students could use as the basis for a talk. Cut a sheet of A4 paper into eight pieces and write a topic on each piece. You could use Activity Sheet 3.1.1 for this. Place each card face-down on a table at the front of the class. Then, make a list of eight different types of audience and do the same thing. Arrange these cards face-down on another table in front of the class. You could use Activity Sheet 3.3.2 for this, which already includes eight different types of audience. This can be adapted as necessary to best suit the text. Divide the class into groups. Ask one of the students from each group to come up to the front of the class and pick one card from each table. They then read out the topic and the audience that they have selected. The group has one opportunity to veto this selection, if they wish. In which case, they must call out 'veto' and then the student at the front must select another two cards. Every student in the group must then plan their own individual talk based on the topic and audience chosen. They could refer to Activity Sheet 3.1.3 to help them plan their work.

- Alternatively, if students require greater support when planning their talk, they could attempt the activity suggested on page 181 of the Student Book. This activity allows students to present in groups, whilst still making an independent contribution adequate for assessment for this part of the unit. Students must participate in a 'Question Time' style activity based on a literary text they have studied. Speakers will make up a panel of four and the class will act as the audience. The speakers will be given a series of topics or exam questions in advance so that they can plan their responses. These topics could be decided by the class before the event of the talk and different members of the audience could be nominated to ask different questions. Each panel member should lead on a question, providing a full response. Other members of the panel will then have an opportunity to develop or qualify what the first speaker said. Possible questions are given on page 181 of the Student Book.

- Activity Sheet 3.1.4 provides support for a talk on a particular character from a literary text. Students could work in pairs to plan and develop a talk to suit this subject matter before delivering it to the class.

- Students could then take it in turns to record the talk based on a literary text using the Record and Playback software provided with the OxBox, (Record and Playback 3.1.3). A number of responses could then be selected at random from the finished recordings. These could be played to the class and students prompted to provide feedback.

- Explain how students are assessed on their ability to 'interact and respond' as part of the speaking and listening unit of their qualification. Refer to page 183 of the Student Book. Stress that the important thing about this part of the unit is for students to show that they can use speaking and listening skills effectively when working as part of a team. Ask students to work in groups of four or five to select a topic from the list provided on page 183 of the Student Book. Before students engage in discussion about the topic, ask them to think independently for a few minutes about the kind of points they would like to raise. Then ask the groups to get together and carry out a discussion. Following the discussion the group should work as a team to summarize the most important and interesting points raised, so that they can feed these points back to the class.

- For further practice students could set up a panel-based discussion similar to the format used for the party leader's debate in the run up to the 2010 general election. Students could watch clips from this three-part debate online to give them a sense of the format of this type of discussion. They could then refer to page 181 of the Student Book, which explains how to set-up a similar discussion. They could change the focus of the discussion from a literary text to a topical issue, for example: the smoking ban in pubs, arranged marriage or how famous sporting figures are treated by the media. Alternatively, each of the speakers could develop a 'policy' of their own that they would like to see introduced in response to a topical issue. They would then need to express their views and justify their policy in the light of questions from the audience. Activity Sheet 3.1.5 provides a customizable version of the 'Question Time' activity on page 181 that can be modified to focus on any topic. Activity Sheet 3.1.6 provides students with further support for planning this kind of discussion.

- Explain that as part of their speaking and listening assessment, students will be expected to show that they can create and sustain roles. Referring to page 186 of the Student Book, point out that this does not mean students are allowed to stick rigidly to a script. They will be expected to improvise to suit the circumstances of the assessment. This means that students need to be flexible in their roles so that they can adapt what they say and how they act according to what other speakers do during the assessment. Ask students to select a task from page 186 or 187 of the Student Book and develop a response in pairs. Students should decide on: the perspective they are each going to take in the dialogue, how they will convey a sense of character in each case and how they can use body language to enhance the performance. Students could use Record and Playback 3.1.4 to practise their dialogue and then either play a final version of the recording back to the class or perform it live.

- For further support for, and practice with, sustaining roles, students could attempt the scenario provided with Activity Sheet 3.1.7. This activity asks students to take on the role of a person applying for a job at a theme park. They have to prepare for, and take part in, an interview for this job. Students could use Record and Playback 3.1.6 to practise their response to this activity.

A-A* students should...

- speak effectively, highlighting the essential details when communicating a complex and demanding subject-matter
- use a sophisticated range of strategies to suit the context and purpose of the task
- use Standard English confidently and flexibly, employing a range of vocabulary and grammatical structures to best suit the purpose of the task
- listen with concentration throughout, using questions to supplement their understanding of what is said
- demonstrate the ability to influence the direction and content of the talk, through actively developing ideas and challenging assumptions
- encourage the participation of others, resolving differences and moving the talk towards a positive outcome
- create complex characters when speaking in role, sustaining a convincing persona through insightful choices and making full use of dramatic approaches
- demonstrate the ability to respond to complex issues and relationships, whilst in role, in varied formal and informal scenarios.

C-B students should...

- convey and interpret information confidently, emphasizing significant points and issues
- shape talk and non-verbal features to best suit the demands of particular contexts and purposes
- use Standard English appropriately and effectively
- respond thoughtfully and considerately to what they hear, challenging and developing ideas with appropriate questions
- help to structure the discussion by identifying useful outcomes and making purposeful contributions
- create a convincing character when speaking in role, using a range of well-selected verbal and non-verbal techniques
- respond with skill and sensitivity, whilst in role, in a range of situations exploring ideas, issues and relationships.

E-D students should...

- communicate information, viewpoints and feelings effectively
- adapt their talk to suit a variety of situations, using non-verbal features for impact
- use Standard English appropriately, using a range of vocabulary and sentence structures to achieve different purposes
- engage with what is heard through perceptive responses
- listen carefully and move discussions forward by engaging with the ideas of others and making relevant contributions
- use appropriate language choices and gestures to sustain a sense of character
- demonstrate an understanding of relationships and significant issues, whilst in character.

Chapter 3.2 Spoken Language
How to teach GCSE English Language Unit 4 Section B

AO2

- Understand variations in spoken language, explaining why language changes in relation to contexts.
- Evaluate the impact of spoken language choices in their own and others' use.

Introduction to the Controlled Assessment

Students will be assessed on their ability to study spoken language by means of a Controlled Assessment. The Controlled Assessment for Unit 4 is divided into two sections, the first of which deals with speaking and listening and the second of which focuses on the study of spoken language. For the second half of this assessment, students will be required to complete one assignment. The assignment should provide a sustained response to the student's own use of spoken language, or that of others, presented by recording, transcript or recollection. Students will need to submit their response in the form of an essay.

Tasks will be set by WJEC each year and students must attempt one of them. Centres may contextualize these tasks to suit their specific circumstances. Tasks will be provided in the April of the year before candidates are entered for this unit.

Students may work collaboratively during the research and planning stage of the assessment, forming discussion groups and carrying out research together. Teachers may also give general guidance. Students may complete this preparation under limited supervision, but the materials they use must be submitted for assessment and moderation.

The final piece of work must be completed individually under controlled conditions. It is expected that this will last up to two hours. If the writing is to be split over a number of sessions, then all work and research materials must be collected in at the end of each session and stored securely.

The tasks are marked by teachers and will be marked out of 20.

Example spoken language tasks

Tasks will be provided by WJEC, but these can be contextualized to best suit the circumstances of the centre. Tasks may be generic or specific. The tasks that follow are examples of generic tasks:

How spoken language is used in different contexts

Candidates reflect and comment critically on their own and others' uses of language in some of the following situations:

- in the workplace
- on television
- in the classroom
- problem solving (giving directions, explaining a procedure, making decisions).

How spoken language is adapted to different listeners

Candidates explore how their own and others' uses of language is adapted in the contexts of wider language use and variation. The following situations would provide appropriate contexts:

- responding to older or younger listeners
- responding to people in authority
- talking to peers and family
- responding to strangers.

The following questions are examples of specific tasks:

Language use in different contexts

Through recording and transcribing classroom interaction **or** by close observation and note-making, show the importance of questioning skills in the classroom.

How spoken language is adapted to different listeners

In everyday life we adapt our spoken language to meet the expectations of other people. We adapt our speech to suit friends, older family members and younger brothers, sisters or cousins. Through recorded conversations **and/or** through close observation and note-making, show how you adapt and change your vocabulary and voice depending on the listener. Choose two or more different listeners to show the range of your ways of speaking.

Key ideas

- Studying spoken language in this unit may be based on the study of transcripts, audio recordings and recollections of speech:
  - recordings – can be audio only or audio-visual
  - transcripts – a written version of a recording
  - recollections – experiences of spoken language use.
- Differences between writing and speech:
  - one is read and the other is heard
  - written language is built out of full sentences and uses punctuation for emphasis and to clarify meaning
  - spoken language is not structured around full sentences and uses intonation, volume, pace and pauses to create emphasis and to clarify meaning.
- Features of spoken English:
  - unpolished or run-on sentences
  - hesitations, pauses
  - repetitions
  - fillers – words or sound used to fill a pause

- contractions – shortened forms
- colloquial or loose vocabulary
- tag questions.
- Things to keep in mind when reading transcripts:
  - transcripts of prepared speech will show fluent and polished prose without the blips that characterize spontaneous speech
  - it is possible to comment on short items of spoken language – including fillers and pauses
  - consider punctuation.
- Use of spoken language varies according to the context, for example:
  - in the workplace
  - on television
  - in the classroom
  - when problem solving.
- Use of spoken language varies according to the listener, for example:
  - responding to older or younger listeners

Key ideas (continued...)

- ◆ responding to people in authority
- ◆ talking to friends and family
- ◆ responding to 'unfamiliar adults'.
- People will choose to adopt standard and non-standard forms of spoken language according to the context, the purpose and the person or people to whom they are speaking.
- Features of non-standard speech:
  - ◆ negatives – "I won't do nothing"

- ◆ parts of verbs – "I seen her"
- ◆ pronouns – "Look at them boys"
- ◆ comparatives and superlatives – "Sam's more cleverer than me"
- ◆ subject-verb agreements – "There isn't no buses running"
- ◆ prepositions – "come over by here"
- ◆ choice of vocabulary – "wee bairn".

Ideas for starters and plenaries

- Ask students what they understand by the term 'spoken language'. Explore some of the following questions to encourage students to identify what they already know about this topic. What kind of media is produced using spoken language? How can spoken language be recorded? How does spoken language differ from written language? Why are people interested in watching and listening to people talk? What extra information might be discovered through listening to spoken language that might not be apparent in written text?

- Play clips of spoken language to the class, either in the form of audio or video, and ask students to comment on how the speakers in each clip use spoken language. Suggested texts include: interviews with politicians, interviews with celebrities, post-match interviews with sports people, clips from reality TV shows, feedback from judges participating in TV talent competitions, radio phone-ins and public speeches.

- How do people adapt their use of spoken language to communicate with different people? Can students differentiate between their own and others' speech when talking to people of different ages such as toddlers, older teenagers or the elderly? Discuss these questions, and then ask students to role-play different conversations, highlighting language features and vocabulary used. Display Presentation 3.2.7, which includes ideas and tips on what to consider.

- Discuss how evidence and examples of spoken language can be analysed in the form of recordings, transcripts and recollections with reference to page 202 of the Student Book. Divide the class into three groups and ask the first group to consider the advantages of using recordings, the second group to consider the advantages of using transcripts and the third group to think about the advantages of using recollections of speech. In pairs within these groups, students should note down as many ideas as they can. Students should then feed back to the class with their ideas. These ideas could be collated on the whiteboard for further discussion or students could use what they have learnt to complete Activity Sheet 3.2.1.

- Play a selection of clips of spoken language to the class, which illustrate people speaking with a range of different accents. For example, post-match interviews with different football players, vox-pop interviews with members of the public or interviews with celebrities. What do students think about regional accents and 'foreign' accents generally? Talk about their opinions, adding some of their ideas to the whiteboard to help develop the discussion. How are accents perceived and presented in the media? Do they feel that society promotes a sense of favouritism and prejudice towards particular accents?

Lesson ideas

- If students have taken part in work experience, they can use the knowledge they have gained from this directly in their spoken language work. Refer students to page 204 of the Student Book. Ask students to share their experiences with the class in order to answer the questions on this page. How do work colleagues speak and behave towards each other? How do employers and supervisors speak and behave to their employees and the people they manage? Gather as many different examples from 'recollections' as possible and add them to the whiteboard. If students have experience of part-time work then they could refer to this too.

- Presentation 3.2.1 continues the focus on spoken language in the workplace, providing further questions to consider and further topics for discussion. These topics include identifying differences between talk at home and talk in the workplace, how speakers might adapt their talk in order to manage another person and broader issues such as negative talk, small talk, swearing and gossip. Students could consider these topics as a class or work on selected tasks in small groups.

- Direct students to the 'On television' section on page 204 of the Student Book. Ask students to write down the title of a TV programme that they enjoy watching and then think of two things about the way spoken language is used in the programme that helps to make it enjoyable. For example, in the case of sitcom it might be that the characters use a lot of funny catch phrases. In a reality TV show, it might be that the spoken language seems to be unedited and therefore offer a more genuine insight into what the speakers think and feel about things.

- Pick a TV programme of your choice for a more detailed discussion of how spoken language is used on television. If some students haven't seen the programme, you could ask other students in the class to explain what type of programme it is, what the main purpose of it is and who it is aimed at. You could play a clip of the programme to get students focused on it. Discuss the way spoken language is used in the programme. For example: *Britain's Got Talent* - why were Ant and Dec chosen as presenters? Discuss accents, comedy value, script choices and how they interact with judges and contestants. How are the three judges, Simon Cowell, Amanda Holden and Piers Morgan different and what do they each bring to the programme? Students could contribute to this discussion with reference to recollections as well as making direct reference to any clips you show in class. Allow students to choose another programme in groups and consider the same discussion points.

- Presentation 3.2.2 provides further ideas for discussion about the use of spoken language on television. Students could work in groups to research one of these topics and produce a presentation for the class. If possible, encourage them to include multimedia material in their presentations such as stills from TV shows, audio clips or video recordings. Alternatively they could build some drama elements into their work, such as asking a member of the group to play the role of a TV presenter and demonstrate some of the spoken language techniques frequently used on TV.

- Referring to the section headed 'In the classroom' on page 205 of the Student Book, ask students to suggest what they understand by the phrase 'classroom management'. How is this responsibility likely to influence the use of spoken language in the classroom? How is it likely to impact the teacher's use of language? What effect might it have on the way students speak in the classroom? Discuss the technique of questioning, emphasizing how questions can be used for different purposes. Students could look at Presentation 3.2.3 to consolidate their understanding and attempt Interactive 3.2.1, which allows them to match a list of example questions to a list of purposes.

- Divide the class into pairs and give each pair a couple of points to focus on from the list of reasons for using questioning on page 205 of the Student Book. For example: 'to bring the class to order', 'to make polite requests' etc. For each point, ask students to come up with a list of questions that illustrate the use of questioning for this purpose. Students should also note down what situations these questions would be used in. Presentation 3.2.3 contains a copy of the list of reasons from page 205, which can be displayed on the whiteboard. Presentation 3.2.4 contains a list of further, related topics for discussion.

- Display Presentation 3.2.5, which includes images depicting a number of everyday scenarios where people have to use spoken language to solve problems. For each slide, ask students to briefly identify what the situation is and explain how the speakers involved will need to adapt their spoken language in order to communicate effectively. Talk about what is expected of the speaker, the purpose of the dialogue in each case, the audience and the situation. How do these factors affect the way the speaker is likely to use spoken language?

- Ask students to read the section headed 'Problem solving' on page 205 of the Student Book and attempt the activity at the top of page 206. Prompt a number of students to feed their responses back to the class. Discuss these responses. What is difficult about problem solving? What do individuals in class find challenging when using spoken language, for example: making decisions, arguing a point, explaining something, giving directions, and why do they think it is difficult? Is it finding the appropriate vocabulary? Lack of confidence? Lack of information? Or something else? Presentation 3.2.6 includes additional topics for discussion. Students can discuss these topics as a class or work in groups to research a topic in detail before feeding back.

- How do young people speak and behave when talking and responding to people in authority? Begin by asking the class for examples of who they see as 'figures of authority'. Collate their ideas on the whiteboard. Refer students to page 207 of the Student Book. Get examples of situations they have been in that have brought them into contact with some of the people they have mentioned. What happened and how did they react? Divide the class into groups and give each group one of the following topics: nerves, complaining, self-confidence, resisting pressure and courtesy. Ask each group to consider how their topic influences the use of spoken language when communicating with people in authority. Ask each group to feed back their ideas.

- How do young people speak and behave when talking and responding to unfamiliar adults? Ask students to look at page 208 of the Student Book. What do students understand by the term 'unfamiliar adult'? Make a list, as a class, of example scenarios where one of the participants may fit this description. Split the class into small groups and give each group a scenario from those that have been suggested. Ask the groups to role-play the scenario. The rest of the class should make observations about how the participants in the role-play use language. Encourage them to comment on factors such as the vocabulary used, body language, pace, volume and tone. Display Presentation 3.2.8, which provides prompts for each of these factors and ideas for further discussion, such as issues of trust, hospitality, embarrassment, courtesy, small talk and putting people at ease. This can be used in conjunction with Activity Sheet 3.2.2, which provides students with a spider diagram to complete.

- Explain the differences between accent (pronunciation) and dialect (grammar, vocabulary). Ask students to look at pages 208 and 209 of the Student Book. They should note down features of a particular accent and a particular dialect, either based on their own accent/dialect or based on another regional variation. Discuss the difference between dialect and slang. Are features of dialect perceived differently to slang? Is this a fair distinction? List situations where dialect is positive and situations where it is regarded as a weakness. Should people be encouraged to speak more formerly? How do newcomers to a school or locality cope? Divide the class into two teams and organize a class debate. One team should argue in support of preserving regional dialects and greater representation of dialects in the media and the other team will argue in favour of standardization, including the teaching of a standardized non-regional way of speaking in schools. Summarize the key arguments of both sides at the end of the debate.

A-A* students should...

- produce a response that shows a sustained awareness of how spoken language is used, selected and adapted
- show insightful understanding of the factors that influence speakers' language choices and analyse changes and variations in spoken language effectively
- be able to successfully understand and evaluate the effects of variation in spoken language.

C-B students should...

- show a confident awareness of how spoken language is used and adapted
- demonstrate confident understanding of factors that influence speakers' language choices and analyse changes and variations in spoken language successfully
- be able to confidently understand and explain the effects of variation in spoken language successfully.

E-D students should...

- show clear awareness of how spoken language is used and adapted
- demonstrate a clear understanding of factors that influence speakers' language choices and analyse changes and variations in spoken language appropriately
- be able to clearly understand the effects of variation in spoken language.